Knowing Him, Updated Spring 2015

live26.org

PODCAST DOWNLOADS

Download the Knowing Him 50-Day Supplemental Podcasts online at the Sonlife Store. Each podcast supplies commentary and additional thoughts from Mark Edwards and Dann Spader for each of the 50 days. Purchase and download the podcasts online at:

Sonlife.com/store

2:6 GROUP PARTICIPANTS

If you are a participant of a 2:6 Group, you can listen or download the supplemental podcasts for free online (as they are included in your 26Network.com account). Learn more about Live 2:6 at live26.org. If you do have an account, log in and click on "Resources" or go to the following URL:

26Network.com/resources

Also from Sonlife & Moody Publishers:

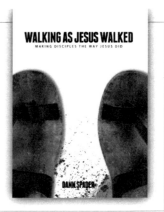

CONTENTS

A Note from the Author

I believe there is no greater endeavor that one can undertake in life than to know Jesus. The Apostle Paul wrote, *"For to me, to live is Christ"* (Phil. 1:27). Paul considered nothing more important: *"I consider everything a loss compared to the surpassing greatness of knowing Christ Jesus my Lord, for whose sake I have lost all things. I consider them rubbish that I may gain Christ"* (Phil. 3:8). I, too, have found nothing in this life that comes close to the joy of knowing Jesus Christ. The passion of my life is to know Him and to yield myself to Him — not just to know facts about Him or know Him as the Savior of the world, but to really connect with Him. I want to have a real relationship with Jesus, not a religion. I wrote this study simply to help you know Him as well. Hopefully, this study will help you to know He who is fully God and fully Man, who had a real earthly family with brothers and sisters, who lived a real life and experienced rejection, hunger, thirst, betrayal, temptation and the joys of being human.

Without a doubt, many throughout history have come to know Jesus better through a chronological study of His life. I have set my heart to study the life of Jesus in a chronological way to enhance my understanding of who God is as revealed through His Son. My mentor Dann Spader launched me into this study of Christ many years ago as a high school senior. He discipled me by sharing with me what he was learning about Jesus. Dann has helped me gain a deep appreciation for both the deity and humanity of Jesus Christ. I share what I have learned over the past thirty years at the urging of friends, and I trust it will challenge your thinking and encourage you to go deeper in knowing Him.

I believe so much in the power of personal exploration that I have designed this study, not to share with you all of my notes and what I have learned, but to help guide you to discover for yourself the greatest person to ever live — Jesus: the Lamb of God who takes away the sin of the world, the Messiah, the Christ, the son of Joseph and Mary, the Jesus of Nazareth, the Lion of the tribe of Judah, the Son of God, the Son of Man.

My heart's desire is that you would fall in love with the Jesus who offered His life as a ransom for you. My hope is that through this study you would not only know more about Him, but that you would truly know Him. I want you to be able to experience life change as He conforms you to the image of His Son.

Please read the next several pages before you jump in, as they will help you understand the four authors. They give us such incredible eyewitness accounts of our Lord's time on Earth, and the man, John the Baptist, who is so intricately tied to the life of our Savior.

I would like to acknowledge the power and work of the Holy Spirit, both in the creation and the development of this study. Without His guidance and encouragement, this study would not have come into being. I would also like to thank several friends who encouraged me to put this study in print. First, there is the person God used to start me on this life-long adventure — my mentor, Dann Spader. My Monday evening disciples — Brian Claus, Eric Gustafson and Jeff McQueary — helped in the fine tuning and editing of this study. My wife Karen constantly provides insight, editing and unconditional love for me. This study is dedicated to all those whom I have discipled, beginning with my own children: JohnMark, Joshua, Rachel and MaryJo; and my brothers, Scott Rolff and Darryl Lawler; and to all those they will disciple in the future. May you make disciples who can then make more disciples until Jesus returns or calls you home.

It is with great joy in my heart that I offer this work on the life of Jesus as a praise offering to God my Father. All the glory is His — He will share it with no man. I simply rejoice that He receives all the glory.

Mark Edwards
Sonlife Latino América
mark.edwards@iteams.org
Google Earth: 10 01'40.78"N 84 03'10.20"W

The Four Gospel Accounts

The Bible that you have is a history book. From beginning to end, this book has one primary focus — to lead the reader in a discovery of who Jesus is. The character of Jesus fills the Bible from cover to cover. When Jesus was on Earth, His strategy was to explain who He was, starting in Genesis and moving through the prophets and the Psalms (Luke 24:27, 44). It is important to understand that the Bible was written by God Himself, that *"All Scripture is God-breathed"* (2 Tim. 3:16). Yet God chose to have men write His words in books, men who *"spoke from God as they were carried along by the Holy Spirit."* (2 Pet. 1:21). God moved in them to write what He wanted using their unique personalities and life perspectives to communicate His truth. What you hold in your hand is *"God-breathed."* It is God's Word, which He supernaturally preserved through the centuries in order that you might be able to understand who He is. There are four eyewitness accounts of the earthly life of Jesus given in the Bible. As you begin this study, it is very important that you consider the purpose behind each book as it relates to the chronology of the life of Jesus.

Matthew (also known as Levi) writes as an eyewitness about much of the life of Jesus. It is important to note that Matthew does not begin following Jesus until Chapter 9 of his book. He is one of the last of the twelve apostles to join Jesus. His occupation was a tax collector, an accountant of sorts. Thus, in Matthew, you can expect to find exact numbers. Matthew is the only author to record the exact amount that Judas received for betraying our Lord (Matt. 26:15).

In his book, it is not really his intent to give us a chronological look at the life of Jesus. Although there is a chronological sequence of sorts in the book of Matthew, it seems that it is more important to write about how Jesus' life impacted his own. **It is the life of Jesus through the eyes of a tax collector from Capernaum.** Many sections are grouped, like the parables of chapters 13 and 25. Even though these parables were probably given on different occasions, they were grouped together by Matthew based on themes.

Mark (also known as John Mark) writes about the life of Jesus. Mark is the scribe, but some believe Peter could be the author. Mark was the son of one of the New Testament Marys, and relative of Barnabas (Col. 4:10). He was most likely discipled by Peter and is made mention of throughout the New Testament. Some believe that Peter was unable to read or write, since he was an uneducated fisherman. Peter has two additional books credited to him, 1 and 2 Peter, although it is believed he did not personally write these books either. Another of his disciples named Silas wrote these two books for him (1 Pet. 5:12). It appears to me that Peter had the advantage of knowing what Matthew's account said prior to writing his own. Thus, in many cases, I think this explains why there are only a few new facts added to the story already shared by Matthew. For instance, you will note Mark simply has three verses on Jesus' baptism and two on his temptation. This is the pattern throughout the book. **Thus, the book of Mark is potentially the life of Jesus through the eyes of an uneducated fisherman.** You will note that most of the events in the book of Mark take place on or around the Sea of Galilee and there are multiple stories about fish.

Luke writes as a first century physician (Col. 4:14). He was most likely born in Antioch and schooled in medicine in Rome. His book will be key for us because he gives us a timeline. In fact, it was the purpose. Luke lays out his intent in the first four verses of his book. *"Inasmuch as many have taken in hand to set in order a narrative of these things which have been fulfilled among us, just as those who from the beginning were eyewitnesses and ministers of the word delivered them to us, it seemed good to me also, having had perfect understanding of all things from the very first **to write to you an orderly account,** most excellent Theophilus; that you may know the certainty of these things in which you were instructed."* (Luke 1:1-4).

These verses tell us clearly that Luke aims to give us a chronological account of the life of Jesus. This book is written to Theophilus, probably a very educated Roman, who has sincere concerns about the order in which events appear in Matthew, as well as the seeming contradictions in the order. There are really no contradictions in Matthew and Mark if you understand that they were not intended to give the chronological account. Also noteworthy is that the book of Luke is written from the eyes of many people, *"eyewitnesses and ministers of the word,"* as Luke puts it, many of who were not the twelve apostles. I believe Mary, the mother of Jesus, is a huge contributor to the book of Luke. It is only in this book that we find the story of the angel coming to Mary and her travels to visit her relatives Zacharias and Elizabeth. There are details here that only Mary could have known. And they are not just in the first two chapters but span the entire book. There is little doubt that Mary was one of the many eyewitnesses that Luke interviewed. **Thus, the book of Luke is the life of Jesus through the eyes of many eyewitnesses, including Mary, the mother of Jesus.** Luke gives us the only true chronological look at the life of Christ. It is for that reason that when there is a question as to the order of events in the life of Jesus, we will always give the most weight to the book of Luke.

John writes the last of the four books, which is dated around 85-90 A.D. John was the youngest of the twelve apostles and outlived all of them. He was the disciple *"whom Jesus loved ... the one who had leaned back against Jesus at the supper"* (John 21:20). John was a fisherman in his youth, the son of Zebedee and brother of

James the apostle. He waited almost 60 years after the death of Jesus to write his gospel. By this time, many had read the gospel accounts of Matthew, Mark and Luke and many questions had risen about Jesus' strategy for His ministry. The first three authors had dedicated very few verses to what John considered to be foundational to a movement of multiplication. In his book, he fills in the gaps of the other authors, painting for us a clearer picture specifically of the first year and a half in the ministry of Jesus. John is also writing to combat false teaching that entered into the church concerning the humanity and deity of Jesus.

Many had begun to believe that Jesus was not a good example to follow because He was fully God and therefore could not have been fully Man. Not wanting to be misunderstood or to be labeled as not believing in the deity of Jesus, John begins his letter with an elegant declaration of the deity of Jesus Christ, declaring Jesus' equality with God, His role in creation, His all-sustaining power and His timelessness. Then, for the next twenty-one chapters, he argues Jesus' humanity. John saw the real Jesus, fully God and yet fully human. John reveals to us the dependent relationship between Jesus and the Father, where Jesus lived by faith in the Father, moment by moment. He stresses the fact that Jesus does nothing on His own initiative but only speaks and moves as the Father prompts Him to (John 5:19; 6:38; 14:10). **Thus, the book of John is the life of Jesus through the eyes of the disciple whom Jesus loved**. John fills in the gaps and gives us the inside track on the human side of Jesus.

This information is crucial when it comes to looking at the life of Jesus chronologically. Equally significant is an understanding of the Jewish culture during Jesus' day, some of which we will touch on in the course of this study. The land on which Jesus walked is also very significant and will shed light on the events as they unfold. I have included a map of the area with the key cities that are mentioned in each section. Take time as you study to trace Jesus' steps. Enjoy!

John the Baptist

The importance of John the Baptist to the study of the life of Jesus cannot be underestimated.

The Old Testament points to John the Baptist as *"A voice of one calling: "In the desert prepare the way for the Lord; make straight in the wilderness a highway for our God""* (Isa. 40:3).

For 400 years, God had been silent. In the closing words of the last book of the Old Testament, God says, ***"See, I will send you the prophet Elijah*** *before that great and dreadful day of the Lord comes. He will turn the hearts of the fathers to their children, and the hearts of the children to their fathers; or else I will come and strike the land with a curse."* (Mal. 4:5-6).

The New Testament opens 400 years later with the appearance of the angel Gabriel, who has come to tell the priest, Zechariah, that he and Elizabeth, his aging wife, will have a son. And the angel says, *"'Do not be afraid, Zechariah; your prayer has been heard. Your wife Elizabeth will bear you a son, and you are to give him the name John. He will be a joy and delight to you, and many will rejoice because of his birth, for he will be great in the sight of the Lord. He is never to take wine or other fermented drink, and he will be filled with the Holy Spirit even from birth. Many of the people of Israel will he bring back to the Lord their God. And **he will go on before the Lord, in the spirit and power of Elijah,** to turn the hearts of fathers to their children and the disobedient to the wisdom of the righteous — to make ready a people prepared for the Lord.'"* (Luke 1:13-17).

The foretelling of the birth of John the Baptist breaks the years of silence — John was the Elijah who was to come. Jesus makes this abundantly clear when He says, *"And if you are willing to accept it, he [John] is the Elijah who was to come."* (Matt. 11:14). This is made even more clear in Matthew 17:11-13. John's tie to Jesus is not simply as a member of his extended family (Luke 1:36), but as his best friend (John 3:27-29) and the first one to understand Jesus' mission as the Lamb of God (John 1:29). Knowing about John is critical to an understanding of the life of Jesus. John plays no small role in Jesus' life and ministry.

Knowing Him

Come join a growing number of disciples of Jesus Christ who believe that Jesus not only came to save us from our sins and provide us a **way** to heaven, but also to reveal Himself as the **truth** and to show us how to really live **life**. For He said, *"'I am the way and the truth and the life.'"* (John 14:6).

The Father is hard at work transforming each of us into the image of His dear Son (Rom. 8:29). It is my prayer that this 50-day adventure in the life of Jesus Christ would aid in the transformation process of Christ being formed in you (Gal. 4:19). My desire is that you might know Him more intimately — as well as the power of His resurrection and the fellowship of His suffering — while being made like Him in all things (Phil. 3:10).

I hope you will be able to say, with thousands of like-minded disciples throughout history, *"For to me, to live is Christ"* (Phil. 1:21); and *"I have been crucified with Christ and I no longer live, but Christ lives in me. The life I live in the body, I live by faith in the Son of God, who loved me and gave himself for me."* (Gal. 2:20).

Come on an adventure that will take your breath away, the adventure of a lifetime. Come on an adventure of **knowing Him.** In fact, you were given eternal life so that you could pursue this adventure: *"Now this is eternal life: that they may know you, the only true God, and Jesus Christ, whom you have sent."* (John 17:3).

Each day, we will be on the lookout to discover both the humanity and the deity of Jesus Christ. This incredible truth can be seen in the duality of His many names: Jesus (humanity) and Christ (deity); Son of Man (humanity) and Son of God (deity); Lion of the tribe of Judah (humanity) and Lamb of God (deity); etc. Unfortunately, little work has been done to help us grapple with the truth that Jesus was fully human and fully God. Yet one cannot escape this reality while studying the earthly life of our Lord. He was made like us in every way (Heb. 2:17), tempted in all things but without sin (Heb. 4:15). He was hungry (Luke 4:2); He was weary and thirsty (John 4:6); He was deeply moved and troubled and even wept (John 11:33,35). What beauty, what mystery we find in the incarnation — God became flesh. God placed Himself in human form, taking on the very form of a servant, being made in likeness as a man, humbling Himself by becoming obedient to the point of death, even death on a cross (Phil. 2:7-8). Come and find the God who became fully man, through the person of Jesus Christ.

Getting Started

The goal of a quiet time is to know God! It is that simple and that profound.

God loves you and desperately wants a personal relationship with you. God is a loving Father who wants to spend time with you. He wants to hear your concerns and show you who He really is and how He can meet your needs. I do not know a fruitful disciple of Christ who does not meet with the Father each day. A daily quiet time with God is more than just a good idea — it is absolutely vital if you are to grow spiritually in Christ.

The plan is simple.

Each day you need to set aside time in your schedule to spend time with God. Consider the example of Jesus:

"Very early in the morning, while it was still dark, Jesus got up, left the house and went off to a solitary place, where He prayed." (Mark 1:35)

Decide on a place and time. Find a quiet spot. It should be away from any distractions.

Then get away by yourself. Bring only your Bible, this study guide and a pen. Get comfortable and prepare to listen to your Father.

Listen first and then — obey!

Each day, pray, *"Abba Father, I want to hear from You today. I am willing to listen and obey. Please speak to me."* Then open His Word and prepare to hear from Him as you read. As you end your study, go through your day determined to obey Him in any circumstance!

You will be asked to apply what you are learning and then share it with another person each day. So, take a moment and think of two people in your life who need to know more about Jesus. Have two in mind? Write their names below:

I will share what I am learning about Jesus with:

_____

_____

I also have included a section in this study called Seeing God. I would encourage you to take time each day to write down where you saw God working in your life. Simply review your day and identify where you saw God at work. This will be an incredible encouragement as you work through this study.

> "Now this is eternal life: that they may know you, the only true God, and Jesus Christ, whom you have sent."
> *John 17:3*

> "I want you to show love, not offer sacrifices. I want you to know me, more than I want burnt offerings."
> *Hosea 6:6 NLT*

50 DAYS

A Study of the Life of Jesus

Preparation Period: Days 1–5

Preparing for a Life of Multiplication

Our study will begin with the birth of Jesus and go all the way to His death, resurrection and ascension. In this first phase of the movement, we will be looking at how the Father prepared His Son to be the greatest leader that has ever lived on Earth. In King David, Jesus gives us a model of how to lead with integrity and skillful hands.

"And David shepherded them with integrity of heart; with skillful hands held them." (Psa. 78:72)

The Father will spend the first thirty years of Jesus' life preparing Him to be the leader and shepherd of His people. The Father will mold Jesus into a man of integrity with skillful hands like He did for David of old.

As we open the pages of the New Testament, we see that the people were awaiting a Messiah, a deliverer to free them from the strong hand of the Roman Empire. They were awaiting the promise made to Moses and their forefathers.

"'I will raise up for them a prophet like you [Moses] from among their brothers; I will put my words in his mouth, and he will tell them everything I command him.'" (Deut. 18:18)

God made a promise for a deliverer like Moses. Yet, before this deliverer would come, there would be one who would come before to proclaim the Day of the Lord and prepare the way for the coming Messiah. He would be like Elijah, the prophet of old.

"See, I will send you the prophet Elijah before that great and dreadful day of the Lord comes." (Mal. 4:5)

Israel was waiting for Elijah to appear and then the Messiah would come and strike fear in the hearts of the enemy and return Israel to her glory.

As the people were anxiously anticipating the coming of Elijah the prophet, God stepped out of heaven's splendor and entered our sinful world as a human — not as a man, but as a baby! Jesus became flesh and lived with us (John 1:14). God, in the form of Jesus, emptied Himself and took on the form of a man.

"Your attitude should be the same as that of Christ Jesus: who, being in the very nature God, did not consider equality with God something to be grasped, but made himself nothing, taking the very nature of a servant, being made in human likeness. And being found in appearance as a man, he humbled himself to death — even death on a cross!" (Phil. 2:5-8)

He was made like us in every way (Heb. 2:17). He came as the Lamb of God to take away the sin of the world (John 1:29).

Come, take a look at the God who was willing to become a man. Fall in love with a God who is so in love with you that He would do whatever it takes to bring you into a personal relationship with Him — even becoming a man Himself.

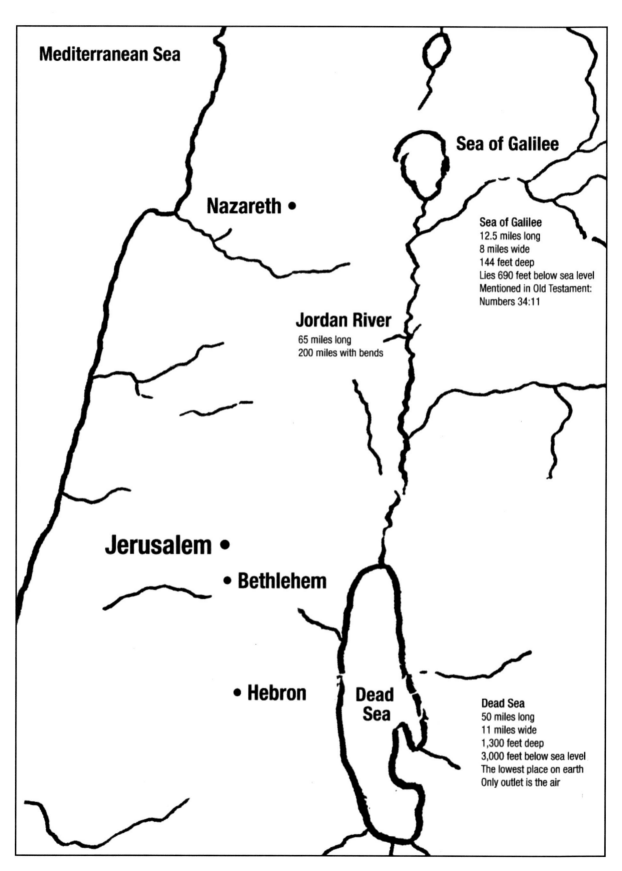

Mediterranean Sea

Sea of Galilee

Nazareth •

Sea of Galilee
12.5 miles long
8 miles wide
144 feet deep
Lies 690 feet below sea level
Mentioned in Old Testament:
Numbers 34:11

Jordan River
65 miles long
200 miles with bends

Jerusalem •

• Bethlehem

• Hebron

Dead Sea

Dead Sea
50 miles long
11 miles wide
1,300 feet deep
3,000 feet below sea level
The lowest place on earth
Only outlet is the air

CHRONOLOGY

Preparing for a Life of Multiplication

The angel foretells of Jesus' birth	Luke 1:26–38
Mary goes to visit Elizabeth	Luke 1:39–40
Mary arrives and John leaps	Luke 1:41–45
Mary returns to Nazareth after staying 3 months	Luke 1:56
The birth of John	Luke 1:57
John circumcised and named	Luke 1:59–63
Zacharias' prophecy	Luke 1:67–79
The angel appears to Joseph; The couple gets married in Nazareth	Matthew 1:18–25
Joseph takes Mary to Bethlehem	Luke 2:1–5
Jesus is born in a feeding trough	Luke 2:6–7
Shepherds see an angel and worship Jesus; Mary tells no one	Luke 2:8–20
Jesus circumcised and named	Luke 2:21
Jesus' first trip to Jerusalem	Luke 2:22–24
Simeon holds Jesus	Luke 2:25–35
Anna prophecies	Luke 2:36–38
Wise men come for a visit	Matthew 2:1–12
Family flees to Egypt	Matthew 2:13–15
Herod kills babies	Matthew 2:16
The angel appears to Joseph; Family returns to Nazareth	Matthew 2:19–23
Jesus grows strong, increasing in wisdom; God's grace is on Him	Luke 2:40
Jesus stays in Jerusalem, full of questions	Luke 2:41–47
Jesus returns to Nazareth; Mary tells no one	Luke 2:51–52
Jesus' teens and 20s	Luke 2:41, 52; Psalm 69:7–12; Isaiah 53:1–5

DAY 1 | Jesus as a Baby

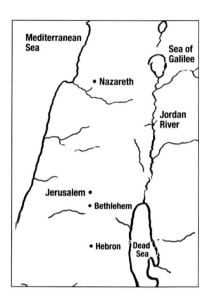

Each day we will be looking deep into the life of the God/Man — Jesus. We will be walking through the 33 years of the earthly life of our Lord. Let's begin by looking at Jesus' first look at the world. Start your time asking God to open the eyes of your understanding as He did for those first disciples: *"Then he opened their minds so they could understand the Scriptures"* (Luke 24:45).

Read the following passages and jot down your questions and observations.

Luke 2:1-20; Matthew 1:1-25; John 1:1-18

As God took on the form of man in Jesus, what are some things He was experiencing for the first time?

When Jesus became a man and walked on earth, He temporarily and voluntarily chose not to exercise the use of His omnipresence (ability to be everywhere at once). What are some other things that Jesus had to give up in order to be human?

What was God's motivation for becoming flesh and blood?

What other questions do you still have?

Outside the Box

God became man! Is there any thought more strange or foreign than that? God Almighty took on human form and entered our world. He chose to begin as a baby and not as a grown man. The Bible says that He *"made himself nothing"* (Phil. 2:7) and put on a body to live here with us. However, He never ceased to be fully God. He was still all-powerful, all-knowing, all-present. Yet He veiled His deity and intentionally limited Himself and His powers to become a real human. He was made like us in every way (Heb. 2:17).

Jesus leaves heaven's glory for earth's insignificance. What a sacrifice on God's part to become one of us! The Creator enters creation, so that He might not only be our God, but also our high priest (Heb. 2:17) and our way to God (John 14:6). What a strange and unusual way to save the world. God's gift to us was a baby.

Have you ever thought about the many gifts God the Father gave His Son, Jesus, on the night that He was born? I am a dad, and I love giving gifts to my children. God is a much lot better dad than I am. I wonder what gifts He might have given. Think about it for a moment. You read about them, but maybe never recognized them as gifts.

How about the gift of a name? God said to call him **Jesus** (Matt.1:21) and that it will be "the name that is above every name, that at the name of Jesus every knee should bow" (Phil. 2:9-10). There is nothing like a good name (Prov. 22:1)!

Wow! Can you think of any other gifts? Jot them down:

Here are some that I thought of:

He received the gift of obedient parents. Mary and Joseph were incredible parents. They did just what God asked them to do. God tells Mary that she would have a baby, even though she had never slept with a man. She said, *"'May it be to me as you have said'"* (Luke 1:38). God says to name Him Jesus and Mary says "Done." And Joseph? God says, *"'Joseph, son of David, do not be afraid to take Mary home as your wife ...'"* (Matt. 1:20). Joseph gets up and marries a pregnant woman, who is bearing a child that is not his. God says, "Call Him Jesus" (Matt. 1:21) and he agrees too. Wow! You know the best gift you can give to the people in your life — your kids, your parents, your friends or whomever — is to be obedient.

There was the gift of a place to be born, a manger outside an inn. Wait, what kind of a gift is that? Well, it was one of the most special gifts that God the Father gave Jesus. Think about the people who probably asked Jesus to tell them about where he was born. "Well, friends, I was born in a manger outside an inn because there was no room for my family," he would reply. Can you hear the laughter? What was God thinking of? Why subject His Son to such humiliation? The answer may possibly be found in Hebrews 5:8. Take a look and dig a little deeper.

Sunrise from on High

"He came as a witness to testify concerning that light, so that through him all men might believe."

John 1:7

Personal Notes

SEEING GOD

Some other gifts:

The gift of a birth announcement and possibly a song, sung by angels (Luke 2:9-14). I wonder how long they practiced in heaven for that performance!

The gift of a star (Matthew 2:2-10). Where did that star go? If it's still around, I wonder which one it is.

The gift of a family (Mark 6:3). Wouldn't that have been something to be an earthly brother or sister of Jesus, to grow up under the same roof?

Live It Out

What gifts has God your Father given you? Make a list.

Spend some time thanking Him for these gifts and specifically for becoming flesh and blood for you, then go out today and share what you discovered with at least two other people.

Other Thoughts

Digging Deeper

Philippians 2:5-11

Hebrews 2:14-18

Hebrews 4:14-16

Hebrews 5:7-14

Hebrews 10:19-25

How much older was John the Baptist than Jesus?

How long did it take Mary to go down from Nazareth to visit Elizabeth? Where did Elizabeth live (Luke 1)? How long did Mary stay with Elizabeth (Luke 1:56)?

What can we learn by looking at the two lineages of Jesus in Matthew and Luke (Matthew 1:2-16; Luke 3:23-38)?

Is there any significance that the first people to meet Jesus were shepherds? There are several shepherds in Jesus' lineage, like David and Jacob.

List the women in Jesus' ancestry (Matthew 1:3,5,6).

What do you think it felt like for Mary to hold her baby boy for the very first time?

Why was Jesus born in a manger?

DAY 2 | Jesus as a Child

Joseph and Mary took the baby Jesus and went to look for family in the Judean Hills of Bethlehem. Remember, this is the land of both their families, which is why they had returned here for the worldwide census, issued by Caesar Augustus. Jesus' family was going to settle in and remain in Bethlehem for a while. We know this because when the wise men came they found the **child** Jesus and not the baby Jesus. They also found Jesus in a house, not a stable (Matt. 2:11). All this you will discover today.

Read the following passage and jot down your questions and observations.
Matthew 2:1-18.

How did Mary and Joseph feel when the wise men came? How many were there? What were the gifts they gave?

Why would the gifts mentioned be appropriate for a king?

How do you see the Father's provision and protection for His Son?

What other questions do you still have?

Outside the Box

On the night Jesus was born, God the Father placed a new star in the sky. This star would eventually lead some wise men from the east to the place where Jesus was living. Can you imagine the preparation that would have gone into taking a journey to a faraway land to visit a newly born king? It must have taken them months to prepare for the journey! Surely in those days they would have brought along servants and guards to protect them, especially when they were carrying such expensive gifts. We can estimate that it took them several months to prepare and make the journey all the way to Bethlehem. We also know that they found Jesus in His home and that He was no longer a baby, but a child. Many suggest that a baby becomes a child when he/she stops breast-feeding. Others believe that it was when a baby turned two. Either way, there is little possibility that the wise men saw Jesus in the stable like many Christmas pictures depict.

"Then they opened their treasures and presented him with gifts of gold and of incense and of myrrh." (Matt. 2:11)

I wonder why God the Father sent kings from a faraway country? What were these gifts to be used for? Think about it and jot down some thoughts.

How much do you think they were worth? What could they have bought in Jesus' day? What did Joseph and Mary do with the gifts? Are the gifts still around today in some cave hidden away, or have they been used up? So many questions!

Some have suggested that the gifts were used to make the family trip down to Egypt. After all, how could the family afford to make such an expensive journey to such a distant land? Others have suggested that Joseph and Mary used the money to give Jesus a top-notch education in Egypt at the university of Alexandria, the leading educational facility in the days of Jesus. After all, Jesus could read, write and speak at least three languages. Where did He learn all this, if not in Egypt? Still others have suggested that the gifts were saved by Mary and used slowly during Jesus' life.

I think it makes the most sense that the gifts were sent by God the Father to be the provision for the family on the journey to Egypt and for their stay there, however long it might have been. But regardless, the thing I don't want you to miss is the fact that God always provided for His Son Jesus. God always provides for His children. Sometimes the provision comes the night before you will need it, sometimes days before and sometimes as you are walking by faith where God is leading you. One of the great names for God the Father is Jehovah-Jireh — *the God who provides.*

The Child

"On coming to the house, they saw the child with his mother Mary, and they bowed down and worshiped him. Then they opened their treasures and presented him with gifts of gold and of incense and of myrrh."

Matthew 2:11

Personal Notes

SEEING GOD

Live It Out

Take some time to think about how God has provided for you throughout your life — things like education, food and work. How is He providing for you right now? Today? Make a list of a few ways.

Spend a few minutes just praising Him for His constant provision for you, then go out and share what you have discovered with at least two other people.

Other Thoughts

Digging Deeper

Exodus 2:1-10

Exodus 4:22-23

Numbers 24:8

Jeremiah 31:15

Hosea 11:1

Who from the Old Testament was saved from a childhood slaughter in Egypt? How does his life parallel that of Jesus (Exod. 2:1-10)?

Compare being born in a manger with being lavished with treasures from foreign kings. What was God saying?

What Old Testament prophecy was fulfilled by God sending Jesus to Egypt?

DAY 3 | Jesus as a Boy

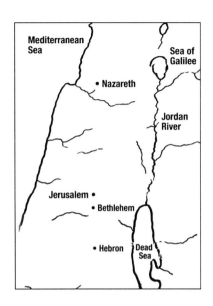

When we left the story yesterday, the Magi (wise men) had just visited Jesus and His family and had brought Him some very expensive gifts. During the night, His father had a dream in which the angel of the Lord appeared to him and said, *"'Get up, take the child and his mother and escape to Egypt'"* (Matt. 2:13). Although we do not know how long Jesus was in Egypt, or all the reasons His heavenly Father took Him there, we do know it was a formative time in His life. Surely Jesus was confronted by people of other cultures and was persecuted for being Jewish in a place that was never friendly to Jews and had a history of bondage and slavery. It was probably not the place Joseph would have chosen for his new family. Maybe Jesus even received several years of education in Egypt, much like Moses did. What will happen to this family next? Today, we will meet the *boy Jesus* as His family makes their yearly pilgrimage to Jerusalem. Come and see.

Read the following passages and jot down your questions and observations.
Luke 2:39-52; Matthew 2:19-23

In what areas did Jesus grow as a human being?

In the Q and A with the religious leaders what was Jesus doing?

Do you think Jesus was teaching the religious leaders or was He learning from them?

What other questions do you still have?

The Boy

"After the Feast was over, while his parents were returning home, the boy Jesus stayed behind in Jerusalem, but they were unaware of it."

Luke 2:43

Personal Notes

Outside the Box

As the family leaves Egypt and heads back to Israel, Joseph is once again directed in a dream to move the family to Nazareth. But why Nazareth? What good could possibly be awaiting the family in Nazareth? Everyone in Nazareth must have known about Mary and Joseph's "situation," with the quick marriage. But it is not just about Joseph and Mary's plans for Jesus, but about God's as well. Jesus continues His education, now in the synagogue in Nazareth under the watchful eye of a religious leader. He begins to hunt for answers to the tough questions like "Why do I not have any of the characteristics of my father Joseph and only those of my mother Mary?" (Remember, Joseph never slept with Mary until after Jesus was born (Matt. 1:25).) "Why do I not have my grandfather's name or my father's name?" "Where did this name Jesus come from?" Or maybe even, "Why do the Messiah and I have so much in common?" These are questions that any 12-year-old in Jesus' shoes might wrestle with. Each year Jesus' family would make a pilgrimage to Jerusalem to celebrate the Passover with family and friends. This year was special — Jesus was now twelve and could ask questions and interact with the religious leaders of His day.

"After three days they found him in the temple courts, sitting among the teachers, listening to them and asking them questions" (Luke 2:46).

I wonder what kinds of things they were talking about. What kinds of questions was Jesus asking them and what were their responses? Oh, to be a fly on the wall that day! I suspect that maybe Jesus as a 12-year-old was beginning to put some pieces together.

Maybe the conversation went something like this:

Jesus: Is it true that the Messiah will be born in Bethlehem of Judah?

Teachers: Yes, of course, young lad, all good Jews know that it is written in Micah 5:2, *"But you, Bethlehem Ephrathah, though you are small among the clans of Judah, out of you will come for me one who will be ruler over Israel"*

Jesus: But isn't it also true that the Messiah will come forth out of Egypt?

Teachers: Silly boy, we just told you that He would come forth out of Bethlehem! How could He come out of two places?

Old priest from the back: Now, hold on a minute, I believe the boy has a legitimate question. Yes, I believe it is true. Look, right here — it is written in Hosea 11:1, *"... and out of Egypt I called My son."* (All are astonished.)

Jesus: So, what if the Messiah was born in Bethlehem and then, for some strange reason, His family had to move to Egypt for a time and then they returned. Could that be a possible explanation for the two scriptures? (All are amazed.) You know, I was born in Bethlehem and then my family moved to Egypt for awhile.

Live It Out

The Bible says, *"Everyone who heard him was amazed at his understanding and his answers"* (Luke 2:47). Have you ever been amazed by Jesus? One thing that I find amazing about this time in Jesus' life is what it says in these two verses: *"And the child grew and became strong; he was filled with wisdom, and the grace of God was upon him"* (Luke 2:40) and *"Jesus grew in wisdom and stature, and in favor with God and men"* (Luke 2:52).

Talk about the humanity of Jesus! It sounds like He was growing in every area of life, just like we do. To those around Him, like His family and these elders/teachers, He certainly looked, sounded and acted human. Maybe it was because He was fully human. What an amazing thing that our God would become like us.

Spend a few minutes just praising Him for becoming fully human, then go out and share what you discovered with at least two other people.

Other Thoughts

Digging Deeper

Since Luke used only eyewitness accounts, who might have been his witness for this event?

What would it have been like to be Jesus' younger brother or sister?

When did Jesus come to the realization that Joseph was not His real father, since by age 12 He was referring to the temple as His "Father's house" (Luke 2:49)?

What temptations might Jesus have gone through as a teen, since we know he was tempted (Heb. 2:17-18; Heb. 4:15)?

What did Mary go through while Jesus was missing for three days (Luke 2:44-48)?

What do we know from the Old Testament about Jesus' growing up years?
Psalm 69:7-9

Isaiah 11:1-5

Hosea 11:1

Micah 5:2

DAY 4 | Jesus as a Young Man

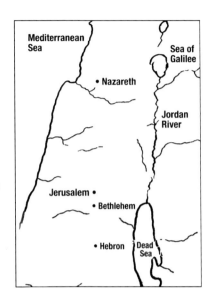

Today, we will be leaving the gospels and looking at an Old Testament Messianic passage. A Messianic passage is a section of scripture in the Old Testament in which God shines light on the coming Messiah, giving people a view of what is to come. We will be doing this from time to time because, really, the whole of the Bible is about Jesus. I remember when my mentor first shared this passage with me and what a huge insight into the growing-up years of Jesus it was for me. In Isaiah, we get a great description of the Messiah that may be unlike anything you would expect! There are great things to be learned, so let's start exploring.

Read the following passage and jot down your questions and observations about each of the three areas.

Isaiah 52:13-53:12

What were some of Jesus' physical attributes? In what other ways does this passage show Jesus' humanity?

How do you see the deity of Jesus in these verses?

How did Jesus suffer, perhaps even as a teenager?

What other questions do you still have?

Arm of the Lord

"Who has believed our message and to whom has the arm of the LORD been revealed?"

Isaiah 53:1

Personal Notes

Outside the Box

Did you catch the new name for Jesus in the first verse of chapter 53? The *"arm of the LORD"* — wow, what a mental image! I see God the Father reaching down to Earth, extending His arm, and that arm is Jesus. God the Creator extends His arm to me in friendship. When I was His enemy and far from Him, He took the first step to reach down in love to give friendship and reconciliation through Jesus. Unbelievable! This passage starts out by talking about the fact that Jesus would grow up in the dry ground of Israel. It was dry in the spiritual sense with hard ground and people with hearts hardened to God. Jesus came to earth and grew up in the midst of a generation hardened to the things of God.

In this passage we get a close-up of what Jesus will look like physically. Did you catch it? Read it again.

"He had no beauty or majesty to attract us to him" (Isa. 53:2).

Jesus wasn't beautiful to look at, nor did he have a grand nature, meaning no nose in the air, no strut like a prince raised in a palace, no kingly pomp. He was just an ordinary guy with an ordinary walk. Yes, he was still a king — the King of Kings. Jesus was royalty, but He left all that behind to become like us in every way. *"Therefore He had to be made like His brothers in all things"* (Heb. 2:17). He was like us in that He grew up as a baby, went through puberty, made it through the middle school and high school of His day. He was an extraordinary person in an ordinary, everyday body of a Jewish male.

He had *"nothing in his appearance that we should desire him"* (Isa. 53:2). Wow — a less-than-attractive picture of the coming Messiah. There was nothing about Jesus' physical appearance that made him stand out. No Hollywood Jesus here with long, flowing blond hair, blue eyes, long legs, perfectly manicured nails, six-pack and highly toned athletic physique. He was just an ordinary guy, physically speaking. Also, Jesus must have looked like Mary, but how about Joseph? What physical qualities did Jesus possess from His earthly dad? He may have looked a lot like His mom and little like His dad. Do you think that went unnoticed by a bunch of high school guys? Let me assure you after 25 years in youth ministry, high school guys would not have missed this one. I can only imagine the teasing Jesus took, if not rejection, for His looks. There was nothing special about His physique.

But why? Why would God put His Son in an ordinary body? Why not give him an Arnold Schwarzenegger physique? In a world that can be obsessed with physically beautiful people, maybe God wanted to remind us that, *"Man looks at the outward appearance, but the LORD looks at the heart"* (1 Sam. 16:7).

Live It Out

Spend a few minutes just thanking Jesus for coming to live as a human and suffering at the hands of the young men of His day — all for you. Then go out and share what you discovered with at least two other people.

Other Thoughts

SEEING GOD

Digging Deeper

What does it mean that Jesus was made like us in every way (Heb. 2:17-18)?

How did Jesus spend His days as a teenager? Many feel that Psalm 69:7-12 could refer to Jesus' growing up years.

What might Jesus have learned from suffering as a teenager (Heb. 5:8-9)?

During His teen years what might Jesus' relationship with Joseph have been like, knowing that he wasn't His real father?

What do you imagine Jesus' relationship was like with His parents and His siblings?

DAY 5 | Jesus as a Carpenter

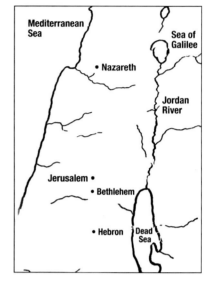

If you had any doubt that Jesus suffered for you after yesterday's study, today's might hit you hard. In Psalms, we get a glimpse into Jesus' relationship with His brothers and His community. The picture is a sad one. It shows what life was like for Jesus on a daily basis. Take a moment to pray before you read God's Word.

Read: Matthew 13:55, Mark 6:3; Psalms 69:7-12.

Many feel that the Messianic Psalms 69, especially verses 7-12, speak of Christ's growing up years. If this is true, what do they tell us about Jesus' early years?

Why would Jesus feel like a stranger and an alien to His brothers (Psa. 69:8)?

Where did Jesus get the strength to endure the suffering? What do you think Jesus was learning from the suffering (Heb. 5:8)?

What other questions do you still have?

Outside the Box

Let me begin today by answering the question, "So, Mark, how do you know that this is a passage about Jesus?" Good question. Grab your Bible and go to John 2:17. In this passage, Jesus is ripping through the temple, defending the honor of His Father's name. Jesus is really mad! When the disciples see Jesus' reaction to the inconsiderate way the temple is being treated, a light bulb goes on in their heads and they have a flashback to when they were little Jewish boys sitting at the feet of the scribes. This is what they learned then: *"'zeal for your house consumes me.'"* Do you remember reading these words? Go back and check out Psalms 69:9. This is one of the ways we know this to be a Messianic passage.

I am not sure what struck you most as you read about these years in Nazareth for Jesus but some of the things that grabbed my heart were that:

- Jesus was dishonored and confused. — Psalms 69:7

- Jesus was a stranger and alien to His brothers. — Psalms 69:8

- Jesus was reproached. — Psalms 69:9-10

- Jesus was a byword, a joke to the people in the community. — Psalms 69:11

- Jesus was the talk of the elders in the city gates. — Psalms 69:12

- Jesus was the song of the drunkards. — Psalms 69:12

Oh, how it must have hurt Jesus to listen to the drunks of His town make fun of Him. And I wonder what the elders at the city gates were saying about Jesus? I imagine they were deciding whose turn it was to talk to Joseph about Jesus' crazy behavior. After all, it does say that Jesus wept, fasted and put on sackcloth. Those are all things Old Testament prophets did when there was sin in Israel. I imagine Jesus might have been walking through town crying over the sin of His people and begging God for mercy on them. Maybe He was even asking His Father to forgive them because they didn't know the mistakes that they were making.

One thing is very clear: Jesus suffered His whole life for you and me. He did not suffer only during the last few hours of His life, but His whole life. *"He was ... a man of sorrows, and familiar with suffering"* (Isa. 53:3). Sit there for a second and let that sink in. Our salvation came at no small price. I have not chosen these verses lightly and in no way do I want to paint a picture of Jesus' growing-up years being completely rotten. Jesus had parents that loved Him, although at times I am sure that Jesus was a puzzle to deal with. Can you imagine having a perfect kid who never sinned? That alone would drive a parent crazy. When people sin around us, it causes us to feel better about our own sin. Not Jesus — He never sinned, He always obeyed and He was always good. All the suffering Jesus faced was undeserved, whereas most of the suffering you and I do is well deserved. Isaiah 53 and Psalms 69 were given to us not to make us to think less of Jesus, but to help us appreciate the sacrifice He made to come and live among us.

Carpenter

"'What's this wisdom that has been given him, that he even does miracles! Isn't this the carpenter?'"
Mark 6:3

Personal Notes

SEEING GOD

Live It Out

Stop today and just think a bit about all Jesus went through for you. Can you believe He would voluntarily do this for you and me? Hard to believe, isn't it?

Spend a few minutes just thanking Jesus for going through that for you, and then go out and share what you discovered with at least two other people.

Other Thoughts

Digging Deeper

What might it have been like to work in the family business?

How would being a carpenter help prepare Jesus for ministry?

How would it have been for Jesus to teach His younger brothers the trade?

Did Jesus have sexual feelings toward women (Heb. 2:18; 4:15)?

What physical infirmities may Jesus have had to wrestle with growing up?

Ministry Foundations: Days 6–15

Building a Strong Root System

The Father spent the first thirty years of Jesus' life preparing Him to be the model leader and the shepherd of His people. Thirty years living as a human being — tempted, suffering, experiencing life growing up in a dry land that was under occupation by a strong Roman force. Jesus was prepared by the Father to emerge as the leader of leaders. There had never been and never will be a leader that is more wise, compassionate and loving as Jesus. He is our model of how to lead and shepherd the flock of God, because He is the Good Shepherd (John 10:11) and the Chief Shepherd (1 Pet. 5:4). If you need a model for leadership, there is none better than Jesus. Read carefully and learn from the Master if you want to learn leadership Jesus-style.

Jesus begins His earthly ministry when He is about thirty years old (Luke 3:23). We call this phase "Ministry Foundations." It lasts about a year and a half. During this time, Jesus will issue two calls. To unbelievers, he says *"Come and see."* To believers, he says *"Follow me"* (John 1:39-40). Jesus calls the masses to come and discover who He is. When they came, He spent time with them, telling them that He is the **way** to heaven (John 3:1-16). He teaches them from Moses, the Psalms and the prophets, then revealed, *"I am the Messiah"* (Luke 24:27-44). He helped them understand the Scriptures and many chose to follow Him (Luke 24:45).

As these believers began to follow Jesus, He continued to explain more of who He was and what was in His heart. He began to model for them the disciplemaking process, which He later commanded them to duplicate (Matt. 28:18-20). Jesus begins to teach them that He is not only the **way** to heaven, but He is the **truth.**

We will look at ten major events in this phase recorded in the four gospels. As you will see, the majority of information about this phase is found in the book of John. In each of those ten events, Jesus is establishing a root system for these new believers. Try to identify the roots as you make your way through. Thus, during this time in the movement, Jesus is evangelizing the unbeliever and edifying the believer. It is important to understand that what Jesus begins to do in this phase, He will continue to do. Even hanging on the cross, He was still evangelizing the unbeliever that hung next to Him and edifying the believers who stood watching.

You will see on the next two pages a map of the places Jesus will visit during this phase and a chronological timeline to help you see the progression of the ministry. As you work your way through the next ten days of this study, I hope you enjoy tracking the growth of Jesus' movement of multiplication. Let's take a look at movement building Jesus-style.

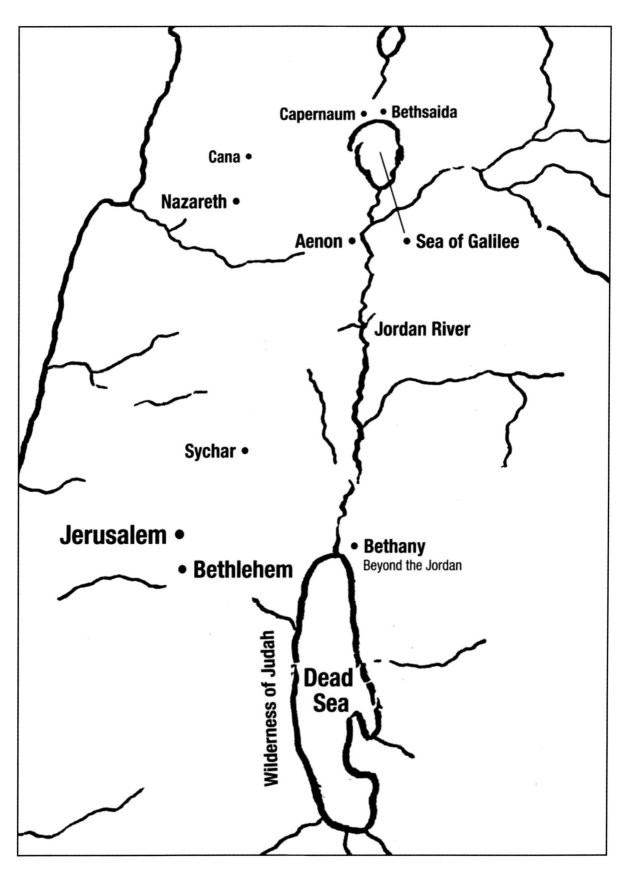

CHRONOLOGY

Modeling Multiplication

John baptizing in Bethany	John 1:28
Jesus baptized by John	Mark 1:9-11
Jesus about 30 years old	Luke 3:23a
Jesus led by the Spirit into the wilderness	Luke 4:1-13; Mark 1:12 and 13; Matthew 4:1-11
Jesus recuperates from fast	Matthew 4:11
John declares "The Lamb of God who takes away the sin of the world"	John 1:29
John sees Jesus in a crowd	John 1:29-34
Jesus calls four disciples	Matthew 4:18-22
Jesus calls Phillip; Phillip finds Nathanael	John 1:43-51
Jesus attends a family wedding and gives first sign	John 2:1-11
Jesus goes to Capernaum with disciples and family	John 2:12
Jesus goes to Jerusalem for Passover	John 2:13
Jesus cleanses the Temple	John 2:14-25
Jesus meets with Nicodemus secretly	John 3:1-21
Jesus' disciples baptize in all Judea	John 4:1-2
John baptizing at the river Aenon	John 3:23-36
Jesus meets a Samaritan woman	John 4:3-26
Great revival in Samaria	John 4:39-42
Jesus welcomed by Galileans	John 4:43-45
Jesus in Cana heals Nobleman's son; Second sign	John 4:46-54
Jesus and family home in Nazareth	Matthew 4:13
John goes to prison	Luke 3:20
John's imprisonment signals a transition	Mark 1:14

DAY 6 | Jesus' Identity Revealed

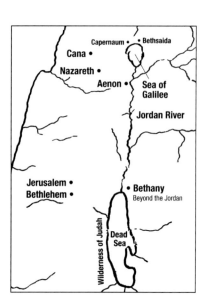

Jesus begins His earthly ministry when He is about thirty years old (Luke 3:23). This first phase of Jesus' earthly ministry will last about a year and a half. Let's look at the circumstances surrounding this momentous occasion. Jesus' ministry starts when the heavens are rolled back and His Father speaks. Wow! What would it have been like to hear God the Father speak? Put yourself in Jesus' sandals today and listen to the Father speak to you.

Read: Luke 3:21-23, Matthew 3:13-17; Mark 1:9-11.

What three things does God the Father reveal about Jesus?

For whose benefit was this revelation?

What would it feel like for Jesus to hear the Father's audible voice after thirty years?

What other questions do you still have?

Outside the Box

Notice the sequence of events: Jesus leaves Nazareth, possibly unsure of His next steps, but feeling confident that the Father is leading Him to visit John. He meets with John and determines that the next step is to be baptized by him. What is this baptism? John said to the people that he was daily baptizing, *"'I baptize you with water. But one more powerful than I will come, the thongs of whose sandals I am not worthy to untie. He will baptize you with the Holy Spirit and with fire'"* (Luke 3:16).

There are many different forms of baptism in the Bible. In this verse alone it mentions three: water, Holy Spirit and fire. It is important to understand what baptism meant in Bible times, especially in Jesus' time. Baptism was used by people to identify with a **messenger** and his **message**. Thus, when people came out to John the Baptist and were baptized they were basically saying, "I believe John is a prophet and a messenger sent from God and I further believe that the words he is speaking, his message of a coming Messiah, is true." When Jesus was baptized, He was saying, "I believe John was sent from God and I believe the message that He is preaching." Baptism is all about **identification,** identifying with Jesus and His message and movement.

After being baptized, Jesus begins to pray (Luke 3:21). Did you catch that small little detail in the story? Jesus begins to talk with His Father. I wonder what He said. Did He ask a question like, "What is next, Father?" Or was He saying, "Here I am, Abba. Send Me!" We do not know, but whatever Jesus was praying, the Father's answer comes quickly and clearly. The heavens open, the Spirit of God descends like a dove and rests on Jesus and the Almighty God says, *"'You are my Son, whom I love; with you I am well pleased'" (Luke 3:22).* Wow! Oh, to hear the voice of God in this way!

What did it feel like for Jesus to hear His Father say these words? They are the words we all long to hear. We were born longing to hear our heavenly Father call us sons and daughters, to tell us He loves us and to hear that He is pleased with us. The words the Father speaks here are words of identity. The first biblical root is that of understanding our true identity. Have you identified with the person and work of Jesus?

Do you understand that at the moment you put your faith in Jesus as your Messiah, you are baptized into Christ? *"For we were all baptized by one Spirit into one body — whether Jews or Greeks, slave or free — and we were all given the one Spirit to drink"* (1 Cor. 12:13). This is the baptism that Jesus came to bring, the baptism of the Spirit. At the moment of your salvation, you were also given a new identity (Gal. 3:26-27; 2 Cor. 5:17). I challenge you to ask questions and dig deeper into your identity in Jesus. This is critical in your growth as a Christ-follower. Allow your identity in Jesus to grow in you. Embrace your new identity as a child of God, deeply loved by Him and well pleasing to Him.

Live It Out

Did you know? You are loved by God (1 John 3:1-3), you are God's child (John 1:12) and God is pleased with you when you put your faith in Him (Heb. 11:6)? Without faith you cannot please God! When you believe by faith that Jesus died for your sins, God is pleased with you and says to you, **"You are My child, I love you and I am pleased with you."**

Spend a few minutes talking with God about your identity. Hear Him say to you, "You are my child, I love you and I am pleased with you." Now go out and share what you discovered with at least two other people.

My Beloved Son

"And a voice from heaven said, 'This is my Son, whom I love; with him I am well pleased.'"

Matthew 3:17

Personal Notes

SEEING GOD

Other Thoughts

Digging Deeper

What do these verses tell us about our identity in Christ?

1 Corinthians 3:16

1 Corinthians 12:27

2 Corinthians 5:17

Galatians 3:26-27

Galatians 4:4-7

Ephesians 2:10

Philippians 3:20

Philippians 4:13

Colossians 2:10

Colossians 3:3

1 John 3:1-3

DAY 7 | Jesus and God's Word

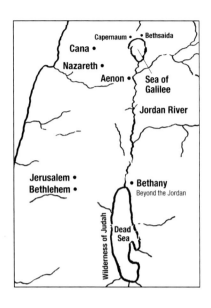

God the Father opens the heavens and speaks to Jesus, telling Him that He loves Him, identifying Him as His Son and telling Him that He is well pleased with Him. What a moment in Jesus' life! Immediately following this event, the Bible says that the Spirit of God led Jesus into the wilderness. Why? What for? What would be waiting for Jesus in the wilderness? Take a look.

Read: Luke 4:1-13; Matthew 4:1-11; Mark 1:12-13.

What is Jesus experiencing physically, mentally, emotionally and spiritually during the forty days in the desert?

Physically:

Mentally:

Emotionally:

Spiritually:

What do you believe was the Father's purpose for leading Jesus into this wilderness experience?

Why do we often need to go through wilderness experiences? See Deuteronomy 8.

What other questions do you still have?

The Lord Your God

"Jesus answered, 'It says: "Do not put the Lord your God to the test."'"

Luke 4:12

Personal Notes

Outside the Box

Jesus was led into the wilderness to be tempted by Satan himself. After forty days of temptations of every kind, the enemy comes again to Jesus. Jesus is now weak, tired and very, very hungry. Notice carefully what Satan says to Jesus.

"'If you are the Son of God, tell these stones to become bread.'" (Matt. 4:3)

The temptation was a direct attack on the truth of God's words. God the Father had just affirmed Jesus' identity as the Son of God at His baptism when He said, *"You are my Son."* Satan then comes and calls into question what God had clearly stated. This has been the devil's strategy from the beginning. Remember when Satan came to Eve, in the form of a serpent, in the Garden of Eden? He said to her, *"'Did God really say, "You must not eat from any tree in the garden"?'"* (Gen. 3:1). Satan is so cunning. He always questions what God has said to get us to doubt the truth. I always remind myself, "Never doubt in the night what God has clearly said in the light."

Satan came to get Jesus to doubt what His Father had just said to Him. Satan offers things that are temporal, things that will satisfy our hunger for the moment but will leave us feeling empty, things that will steal the Word of God from us and attack our new identity in Christ. Satan loves to attack the Word of God because he knows if we doubt what God has said, we will be immobilized and, eventually, become disobedient to God.

Notice how Jesus overcomes the devil. He quotes from the Word of God: *"... man does not live on bread alone but on every word that comes from out of the mouth of the LORD."* (Deut. 8:3). Jesus uses the Word of God to overcome the attack on His identity. The key to overcoming temptation is to know the Word of God. We would be wise to learn from our Master.

Finally, note that this is not the only time in Jesus' life when He was tempted. Near the end of this passage, it says, *"When the devil had finished all this tempting, he left him until an opportune time"* (Luke 4:13). Temptation is a daily thing in the life of all human beings — get used to it. Soak in the Word of God and allow it to purify you (Psa. 119:9). Reading God's Word and meditating on it is like taking a bath — it will purify you and give you confidence to fight back in the face of temptation. When temptation comes knocking at your door, will you be as ready as Jesus was? When the enemy attacks your identity in Jesus, will you be ready with truth from God's Word to strike back? I challenge you to memorize God's Word. It is your sword in the fight against temptation (Eph. 6:17). The Word of God is instrumental: *"For the word of God is living and active. Sharper than any double-edged sword, it penetrates even to dividing soul and spirit, joints and marrow; it judges the thoughts and attitudes of the heart"* (Heb. 4:12). Get the Word of God in your heart and start fighting temptation, instead of yielding to it.

Live It Out

The key to overcoming temptation is to live by every word that God the Father gives us. Have you felt the attack of the enemy this past week? Remember, his goal is to cause you to doubt what God has said to you through His Word. This doubt will lead to unbelief and disobedience. Don't fall into his trap; be like Jesus and immerse yourself in the Word of God. The second root that needs to be established in the life of a Christ-follower is the Word of God.

Spend a few minutes committing these verses about your identity to memory (1 John 3:1; Heb.11:6). Have a conversation with a friend today about temptation and how to overcome it.

Other Thoughts

Digging Deeper

Deuteronomy 8:3

Psalms 1:1-6

Psalms 119:9

Psalms 119:105

Proverbs 30:5

Jeremiah 23:29

John 1:1-18

John 8:32

2 Timothy 2:15

Hebrews 4:12

SEEING GOD

DAY 8 | Come and See; Follow Me

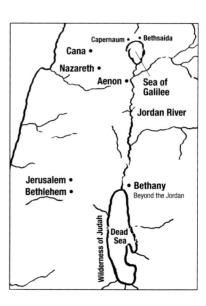

After more than forty days in the wilderness, Jesus comes through the time of temptation and embarks on a mission to start making disciples. He begins by calling people to *"Come and see,"* to come and investigate the facts of who He is. He then opens their eyes to the truth that He is the promised Messiah they have been waiting for. As they believe, He changes His message to *"Follow Me."* Two calls — one to those who have not yet believed and one to those who believe. Notice on the map where Jesus is. He returns to Bethany, on the other side of the Jordan, where John had been baptizing people (John 1:28). There were several towns called Bethany in Jesus' day. One was a few miles outside of Jerusalem, home to Mary and Martha, who we will meet later and another was on the other side of the Jordan River. It is at the latter Bethany that Jesus makes these first two calls, *"Come and see"* and *"Follow Me."* Dive into the story and be on the lookout for words that reveal Jesus' humanity and deity.

Read: John 1:19-51. Jot down what you discover in each of the three areas:

Who is Jesus?

What is Jesus modeling?

What are His new followers experiencing (learning)?

What other questions do you still have?

Outside the Box

After having His identity confirmed by God the Father and then facing the enemy who tried to call into doubt the Word of the Father, Jesus returns to call His first followers. The first call is a simple one: *"Come and you will see"* (John 1:39). John and Andrew decide to check out Jesus and hear what He had to say. They follow him home and spend the evening getting to know Him. What did He tell them? Turn back a few pages in your Bible and read Luke 24:27,32,44 and you will discover an example of what they probably talked about that night.

Jesus' strategy is simple. First, He challenged people to *"Come and see."* Then He would spend time with them and explain to them who He was. Jesus invited these two young men to come and spend time with Him. He simply shared with them who He was, using something they were very familiar with — the writings of Moses, the Psalms and the Prophets. He took them back to their Jewish roots and shared with them that He, Jesus, was the fulfillment of every Old Testament prophesy and He was the long-awaited One — the Messiah. What an experience that must have been!

It is obvious that after spending time with Jesus, these two young men were convinced of the fact that Jesus was indeed the Messiah. We can see this in their enthusiastic acceptance of Jesus' message. Andrew runs to find his brother Peter and says, *"'We have found the Messiah' (that is, the Christ)"* (John 1:41). Andrew then brought his brother to meet Jesus. What a simple plan! It is all about challenging people to come and see who Jesus is. We don't have to argue them into the Kingdom; we can just call them to come and check out Jesus. Some will come and others will not. To those who come, we simply explain who Jesus is in words that they will understand. Using the Word of God, we share what God has said about Jesus and challenge them to confront the truth. That is our job — to take a step of faith to believe that God will open their minds to understand the Scriptures. Check it out in Luke 24:45. At the end of the day, we can call people to *"Come and see";* we can explain clearly from Scripture who Jesus is, but we are ultimately dependent on God to open their minds to the truth and move them to accept Jesus. The third root is telling others about truth of Jesus. In this story, four people give testimony of who Jesus is: **John the Baptist:** *"'Look, the Lamb of God, who takes away the sin of the world!'"* (John 1:29); **Jesus:** *"'Come and you will see'"* (John 1:39); **Andrew:** *"'We have found the Messiah'"* (John 1:41); and **Philip:** *"'We have found the one Moses wrote about in the Law, and about whom the Prophets also wrote — Jesus of Nazareth, the Son of Joseph…Come and see"* (John 1:45-46).

It is interesting how quickly these new followers picked up on Jesus' simple strategy of multiplication. Jesus challenged them to *"Come and see,"* and Andrew and Philip did the same. Andrew called Peter his brother and Philip called his friend Nathanael. The call to follow is the first call that we received and the first call we give those with whom we come in contact with. "Come check out Jesus. Come take a look at the claims of Christ." That is our job. Simply call people to come and see. Not too hard, is it?

Lamb of God

"When he saw Jesus passing by, he said, Look, the Lamb of God!"

John 1:36

Personal Notes

SEEING GOD

Live It Out

Who do you know in your life that needs to know that Jesus is the Messiah, the Savior of the world? Write their name down: _____.

Take a moment and pray for them. Today, your assignment is to contact them, write them or get together for a soda and call them to *"Come and see."* Take a moment and write down your challenge to them. How will you say *"Come and see"* in a language that they will understand?

Now go and call someone to *"Come and see"* and observe how exciting it is to walk through life calling people to check out Jesus. Give it a try. It's fun!

Other Thoughts

Digging Deeper

Genesis 3:14-15

Genesis 17:1-8

Deuteronomy 18:15-18

Isaiah 9:6-7

Isaiah 11:1-2

Isaiah 53:1-12

Micah 5:2

Malachi 4:1-6

DAY 9 | A Real Family

After you have challenged your family and friends to come and check out Jesus, you must begin to explain to them what the Bible says about Him. You must tell them who He is. There is a lot that the Bible says about who Jesus is, so where do you begin? We learned yesterday that Jesus began where the people were, where they would best understand, and He used the Bible — the Word of God. Let's see where He goes from there with this first group of "Christ-followers."

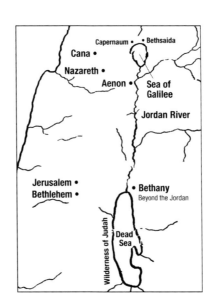

Read: John 2:1-11.

What can we learn about Jesus' priorities from this passage?

What is unique about this miracle?

Mary stated in v. 5, *"'Do whatever he tells you.'"* Why is this great advice from any parent? Do you think Mary was expecting a miracle? Why or why not?

What other questions do you still have?

Son of Mary

"'Where did this man get these things?' they asked. 'What's this wisdom that has been given him, that he even does miracles! Isn't this the carpenter? Isn't this Mary's son and the brother of James, Joseph, Judas and Simon? Aren't his sisters here with us?' And they took offense at him."

Mark 6:3

Personal Notes

Outside the Box

There are key truths about Jesus that one must share with anyone. Jesus will spend the next three years of His life revealing to His followers the truth of who He is. There are many things that He will reveal, each in its own time. He has a well thought-out plan. One of the things that Jesus revealed yesterday to His first followers was His deity and His humanity. Did you pick up on the phrases? Andrew says to Peter: "*We have found the Messiah' (that is, the Christ)*" (John 1:41). Here we see Jesus' deity revealed through the use of the word "Messiah." Then Philip says to Nathaniel, "*We have found the one whom Moses wrote about in the Law, and about whom the Prophets also wrote — Jesus of Nazareth, the son of Joseph*" (John 1:41). The phrase shouts that Jesus is a real person, with a real family, from a real town in Israel.

Jesus challenges them to *"Follow Me."* They follow and get to meet Jesus' family! I imagine them getting a chance to embrace Jesus' mother, shake hands with His brothers and offer a kiss of greeting to His sisters. Can you see Jesus' display of humanity here? He shows that he is fully man. But, then He displays His deity in a supernatural act. He saves the wedding by turning water into wine. Why? Look back at verse 11 for the answer. It says this was His first sign and he did it to manifest His glory. His disciples began to believe that He was who He said He was. They already had believed, but now some of their beliefs were being confirmed. Can you see that as they grew in their knowledge and experience with Jesus that they grew in their faith? Their ability to trust Jesus deepened the more they got to know Him. By getting to meet His actual family and by witnessing His first miracle, they were able to see firsthand His humanity and deity. That is the fourth root — Jesus' humanity and deity, the one who is God and Man at the same time.

So far we have discovered four roots that Jesus is planting in His first followers as He seeks to establish them in this new movement of multiplication. Did you pick them up? Jot down the first four roots:

Root #1 —

Root #2 —

Root #3 —

Root #4 —

Live It Out

The closer those earlier followers got to Jesus, the more they learned about the truth of who He was. It is the same for us today. *"Come near to God and he will come near to you"* (Jam. 4:8). Take some time to draw near to Him. Spend a few minutes thanking God for the gift of His Son. Thank Him that He would expose Himself to sinful men and be tempted in all things like us. Try sharing with someone who needs to go deeper with Jesus. Challenge them to join you in answering the call to *"Follow Me."*

Other Thoughts

Digging Deeper

2 Corinthians 5:21

Philippians 2:5-11

Hebrews 2:14-18

Hebrews 4:14-15

Hebrews 5:7-8

Hebrews 7:26-28

DAY 10 | Passion at the Temple

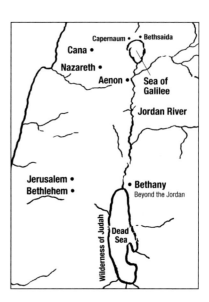

Jesus leaves the wedding ceremony and heads up to Jerusalem with His disciples and family for the feast of the Passover. This seven-day Jewish feast has its roots in God's deliverance of His people from Egypt under the leadership of Moses. Jesus enters the feast and becomes very, very impassioned. What gets Jesus' blood pressure soaring? As you read this story, ask yourself if you are passionate about the same things that Jesus is passionate about.

Read: John 2:12-25.

As you read this passage, what do you see is the message of Jesus?

What were Jesus' priorities here?

What was Jesus modeling for us?

What other questions do you still have?

Outside the Box

As Jesus enters the temple area, He becomes very angry. Yes, God gets angry: *"'God is a consuming fire'"* (Heb. 12:29). Righteous anger is definitely appropriate. Jesus expressed His righteous anger when, *"he made a whip out of cords, and drove all from the temple area, both sheep and cattle; he scattered the coins of the money changers and overturned their tables"* (John 2:15).

This is important because it shows that Jesus did not come into Jerusalem angry and carrying a whip. It shows us that Jesus made a whip. I wonder where he learned that, and from whom? Jesus made this whip when he observed two things happening: one, the selling of sacrificial animals in the temple and two, the exchanging of foreign monies. Why would these two things stir such a passionate response in Jesus? One thing is clear — the focus had been taken off worship of the Father and was placed on an opportunity to make some money. The religious people had seized upon the poor and the foreigners who had come to worship and were exploiting them. They had become opportunists. They saw uneducated men and foreigners, who could be easily manipulated and exploited.

Jesus' first followers watched in stunned amazement as Jesus drove these opportunists from the temple mount, and they remember something they had been taught as young children. They remember the words written in Psalms 69:9 about the Messiah, *"zeal for your [God's] house consumes me.'"* The word "zeal" means zealous, jealous or passionate. It is a stirring deep within a man that causes him to be moved to action. Jesus was jealous of God's name and His reputation. He did not want anything to damage it. He did not want people to think that this selling of animals and exchanging of money had anything to do with a personal relationship with the living God. People were more concerned about the marketing of a religion than having a vibrant relationship with the living God. How easy it is to turn what is meant to be a living relationship into a dead religion. What makes your blood pressure rise? Whose reputation is more important to you, yours or God's? Jesus was consumed with the Father. What consumes you? Make Jesus your consuming thought: His name, His fame and His glory. It is really all about Him and not about us, despite what the world tells us each day.

We see real human emotions here from a real human Jesus; we see real courage here from a real divine Jesus, who was so in love with the Father that He could not stand by and see people make money from what God was offering as a free gift. When questioned about this by the leaders of His day, Jesus responds by saying, *"'Destroy this temple, and I will raise it again in three days'"* (John 2:19). Their eyes were so on themselves and the physical world that they could not see that Jesus was not talking about the temple, but Himself and how He would die and be raised again for us. The question is: where are your eyes today?

Root number five is passion — a passion for His name, His fame and His glory.

The Word

"The Word became flesh and made his dwelling among us. We have seen his glory, the glory of the One and Only, who came from the Father, full of grace and truth."

John 1:14

Personal Notes

SEEING GOD

Live It Out

Jesus was passionate for God's name and fame. What are you passionate about? What cause are you consumed by? Think about a few things that get your blood flowing. Now ask the question: is this what got Jesus' blood flowing? If not, then maybe it is time to consider realigning your passions. Discuss with a friend today what you are jealous, zealous and passionate about. Share what you are learning about Jesus' passion for His Father.

Other Thoughts

Digging Deeper

Deuteronomy 16:1-6

Psalms 69:9

Malachi 3:1-4

1 Corinthians 3:16-23

1 Corinthians 6:19-20

DAY 11 | A Nighttime Look at Jesus

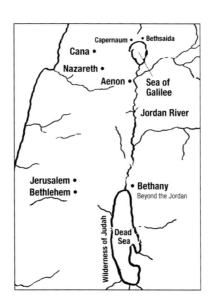

Jesus' display of passion in the temple during the Passover must have raised many eyebrows, but Jesus was then launched onto the stage of popularity in His day. The Bible says, *"When he arrived in Galilee, the Galileans welcomed him. They had seen all that he had done in Jerusalem at the Passover Feast, for they also had been there"* (John 4:45). But before that, Jesus had a meeting with a man named Nicodemus, who was very religious. He was probably one of the people who had most likely seen what Jesus did at the wedding. He comes to meet Jesus under the cover of dark, because he was deeply concerned with his own reputation and did not want to be seen with Jesus. Take a look.

Read: John 3:1-21.

What does this passage tell us about Nicodemus?

What can we learn about Jesus from this passage?

What does this passage tell us about the Kingdom of God?

What other questions do you still have?

Only Begotten Son

"For God so loved the world that he gave his one and only Son, that whoever believes in him shall not perish but have eternal life."

John 3:16

Personal Notes

Outside the Box

Throughout Jesus' ministry we see Him calling people to *"Come and see."* This is the same call that we make to those who do not know yet that Jesus is the Messiah, the Savior of the world. You will note that some people turn and walk away and other people come at different times and in different places with an infectious curiosity. In this nighttime encounter with Jesus, Nicodemus is challenged to take his eyes off of himself long enough to see that the world we live in is not one-dimensional. When people come to Jesus, He will always reveal Himself as the way to heaven like He does here with Nicodemus. I wonder who invited Nicodemus to this garden encounter? Was it Jesus? Could it have possibly been John? Some have suggested that John was related to Nicodemus, maybe a nephew. It is interesting to note that only in the book of John is Nicodemus mentioned. Maybe John's inside connection, which got him in the inner court the night of Jesus' betrayal, was his uncle Nicodemus.

But more importantly, in this encounter we see the Master teaching us how to share who Jesus is with a religious unbeliever. Jesus' strategy is masterful, taking Nicodemus from the seemingly impossible concept of being born again to the possibility, in Christ, of living in the Light free from fear. The process is one of faith. Nicodemus lacks faith. He is looking at everything physically and sees only the impossibility. Read back through the story, noting Jesus' strategy. Jesus challenges Nicodemus to open his eyes of faith. Root number six is faith. You cannot physically see the wind, but you can see its effects as it blows. Just because you cannot see something with your physical eyes, does not mean that it does not exist. Jesus says it is the same for those who have been born in the Spirit (John 3:8). What is not possible to see physically is possible with God because He loved us. He loved us so much that He provided a way to be reborn, to have new life in Him. God's love sent Jesus into His world to be lifted up and then die that we might have an eternal relationship with God the Father, our Creator, through Jesus.

Jesus goes to a very familiar story written by Moses with Nicodemus. It is found in Numbers 21:4-9. If you have time, stop and read the story. In this story, the people rebelled against God and were complaining about God's provision. God allowed poisonous snakes in the camp to bite the people and then told Moses to craft a bronze serpent and place it on a pole. He had to tell the people that those who looked up at the bronze snake, in obedience, would be saved. This was exactly what this religious leader needed to do. He needed to take a step of faith, take his eyes off himself and look to Jesus as his Messiah sent from God. He needed to put His trust in Jesus. Did you see a glimpse of Jesus in the books of Moses? What a strong symbol of what was to happen on the cross. Jesus was to die for our sins, to take away the bite of the serpent Satan, to free us from the venom of sin and heal us. As Jesus hung on the cross, Satan thought he had his victory, but just the opposite was about to take place. On the cross Jesus died, but really it was the death of sin and Satan's grip over us (1 Cor. 15:55-57).

Whatever happened to Nicodemus? Keep your eyes open and we will run into him later in the life of Jesus.

Live It Out

Do you have a friend who has not yet seen with faith past this physical life to the One who can offer the Way to a relationship with God? Spend a few minutes praying for your friend. Then I would challenge you to share who Jesus is with that friend today. Tell your friend that it is possible to be born again and experience a real, authentic relationship with God through Jesus Christ. Challenge them to take their eyes off of themselves and this physical world and look on Jesus, the author and perfecter of faith.

Other Thoughts

Digging Deeper

Numbers 21:4-9

Ecclesiastes 11:5

Ezekiel 36:25-27

John 19:38-42

1 Corinthians 15:50-58

DAY 12 | The Source of Real Joy

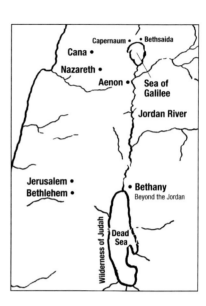

Take a moment and find the River Aenon on the map. Note that the river Aenon is on the border of Samaria. This is a very important place, and we need to ask the question — why was John the Baptist near Samaria? What was he doing there? Up until this time, he had spent his time preparing the way for the Messiah among the Jewish people, like a voice crying in the desert, making straight the path (Isa. 40:3). John had been focused on the Jews, so why is he here near Samaria? And by the way — why did John not leave his ministry of preparing the way and just follow after Jesus like he tells his disciples too? Well, let's see what we can uncover.

Read: John 3:22-35.

Up to this point, what do you know about John the Baptist?

How would you describe John's character?

What is John modeling for us?

What was Jesus modeling for us in John 3:22? In John 4:1-3?

What other questions do you still have?

Outside the Box

Today we have two guys, Jesus and John, meeting at a river to talk about life and ministry. At this river, much of what we learn about Jesus is seen through the eyes of Jesus' best friend. Did you miss that part? Okay, let me paint the picture — at least how I envision this meeting took place. I believe that after John identified Jesus as the Lamb of God (John 1:29), Jesus told John that he needed to continue to prepare the way and that John's work was not yet done. So, Jesus sent John ahead of Him to keep doing what he was doing. This will become clearer tomorrow as we look at Jesus when He comes to the Samaritan people. Jesus and John talk about the next steps in the movement of multiplication and Jesus departs. As Jesus is walking away, John's disciples come to him (v. 26) and want to know why Jesus' ministry is growing and John's is shrinking. Wow! Go back and read verses 27-30 and discover the heart of a real man of God, a real disciple of Jesus. Go ahead.

Here are key points of a man of God from John the Baptist:

One: John knew who he was and who Jesus was. John knew Jesus was the Messiah and that Jesus was the Bridegroom. John knows who he is, the friend of the Bridegroom. In fact, the best man. I believe John the Baptist will one day fulfill the role as Jesus' best man in the great marriage feast of the Lamb (Rev. 19:7-9).

Two: John had discovered the source of real joy and it did not lie in how the ministry was doing or the circumstances of life, but in being next to the Bridegroom and listening to His voice. Don't miss this. John says, *"The bride belongs to the bridegroom. The friend who attends the bridegroom waits and listens for him, and is full of joy when he hears the bridegroom's voice. That joy is mine, and it is now complete"* (John 3:29). John's joy was complete because he stood next to the Bridegroom and heard Him speak. Real joy is only found next to the Bridegroom, listening to His voice.

Third: John knew that after he heard Jesus speak, he could do nothing but obey. John knew that it was all about Jesus and not about him. It is all about being Jesus-centered and not me-centered. John says that he must become less so that Jesus can become more (John 3:30). It is all about dying to ourselves and becoming obedient to His will. John is one of the clearest pictures of a man who has learned to die to self and live to Christ. He found the source of real joy in Jesus.

Live It Out

Root number seven is the priority of being with Jesus and listening to His voice. I cannot tell you how important this is if you are to grow as a true disciple of Jesus Christ, one who is able to make disciples. You must practice the presence of God. You must get before God, listen and obey no matter what. You must die to self and allow Jesus to live through you. Find a friend who knows Jesus and discuss what it means to decrease so that He might increase in you.

Bridegroom

"The bride belongs to the bridegroom. The friend who attends the bridegroom waits and listens for him, and is full of joy when he hears the bridegroom's voice. That joy is mine, and it is now complete."

John 3:29

Personal Notes

SEEING GOD

Other Thoughts

Digging Deeper

Isaiah 40:1-4

Matthew 3:1-12

Luke 1:39-80

John 1:19-34

Galatians 2:20

Revelation 19:7-16

DAY 13 | The Harvest is Ripe

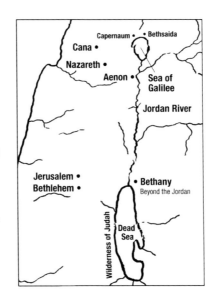

Jesus leaves His best friend John at the River Aenon and heads back down into Judea where He had left His first followers to continue testifying about Him and baptizing the people (John 4:1-3). Do you remember what baptism meant? Jesus' early followers were helping the people to identify with the person and work of Jesus. This was why they were baptizing them. Jesus collects His followers and begins to head back up to Galilee, but first He must pass through Samaria. Look again at the map and get your bearings. Let's go north into Samaria to the town of Sychar.

Read: John 4:1-42.

What does this passage tell you about Jesus' priorities?

What is Jesus modeling?

Where do you see Jesus' humanity?

What other questions do you still have?

Living Water

Personal Notes

Outside the Box

In Jesus' day there was a tremendous hatred and prejudice against the Samaritan people. Did you catch the woman's words in the passage? She said, *"'You are a Jew and I am a Samaritan woman. How can you ask me for a drink?' (For Jews do not associate with Samaritans)"* (John 4:9). Why did the Jews not like the Samaritans? The story goes all the way back to the book of Genesis, and the fact that Israel blessed the two sons of Joseph: Ephraim and Manasseh. These sons were half Egyptian and half Jewish and they were given the land that in Jesus' time was called Samaria. In fact, Joseph should have received one plot of land like all of his other brothers, but his father obviously loved him more and chose to give him the two best plots of land. Thus, Ephraim and Manasseh got huge chunks of the best land.

These two tribes were hated from the beginning and always looked down on by the Jews. If you have some extra time this week, go to the Digging Deeper section and read the history of Joseph. In fact, the place where Jesus is sitting is believed to be the place where Joseph's bones were buried, the ones that had been carried all the way from Egypt (Josh. 24: 32). Wow! Hopefully you can better understand the racial problem that began hundreds of years ago. These problems still exist in that part of the world; there is deep racism and hatred and infighting among people who all trace their roots back to Abraham.

In this story, we see Jesus is breaking two cultural taboos. First, He was speaking to a Samaritan and second, He was speaking to a woman. Another big problem in Jesus' day was prejudice and mistreatment of women. Women were used more than appreciated. For these reasons this conversation catches both the Samaritan woman and Jesus' followers by surprise (John 4:9,27). We see Jesus' humanity in this story when He is both thirsty and hungry. He asks the woman for some water and sends His followers to get some food.

In this story Jesus also states clearly His purpose for coming to Earth: *"'My food,' said Jesus, 'is to do the **will** of him who sent me and to finish his **work**'"* (John 4:34). We learn later that Jesus in His humanity struggled with the will of the Father. But He finally yields and says, *"'... yet not my will, but yours be done"* (Luke 22:42). The will of the Father was for Jesus to die on a cross. But what is the work of the Father? Is it the same? In John 17:4, Jesus says, *"'I have brought you glory on earth by completing the work you gave me to do.'"* He says this before He dies, thus the work must be something different from the will. If Jesus' only purpose for coming to earth was to die on the cross, why then did He not die when He was 12, 18 or 25? Why wait until He was around 33 years old to die on the cross? The reason is because Jesus had to not only complete the will of God, but the work of God as well. The Father's work for him was to prepare some people who would carry the message of His death and resurrection around the world. He was given the task of making disciples who could make disciples. That is the work of Jesus. This is what we are looking at in this study — how to make disciples. Why? Because before Jesus leaves earth, He says to His disciples, *"'As the Father has sent me, I am sending you'"* (John 20:21). God has a will for you and work! What is it?

Live It Out

You and I have a work to do — we must **make disciples** (Matt.28:19). We also have to do the will of the Father. The will of the Father is the same as it was for Jesus — to die. We need to die to self and allow Jesus to live in and through us. Our thoughts should be like Paul's when he said, *"I have been crucified with Christ and I no longer live, but Christ lives in me"* (Gal. 2:20). Paul discovered the secret of the victorious Christian life is having Christ in us, living through us.

We can also gain insight from this story into sharing Jesus with people of other religions. I don't want you to miss this. Notice that Jesus begins the conversation by placing Himself in a position of need. I am thirsty; give me something to drink. Before telling the woman who He is, Jesus first allows Himself to be in a position of needing her help. This is a good model for sharing Jesus with people from other religions. Allow yourself to be in a position of need, asking them for help and then be willing to offer help for their souls.

Other Thoughts

Digging Deeper

Genesis 41:38-46

Genesis 48:8-22

Genesis 50:22-26

Joshua 24:14-32

Hebrews 11:22

DAY 14 | Extreme Faith

As Jesus and His followers leave Samaria and head back into Galilee, the news about Him has already reached the people and the talk in all Israel is about the new prophet on the scene — Jesus of Nazareth. As His hometown tries to sort through their emotions about who Jesus really is and how they could have missed it, Jesus makes His way a little north, to the town of Cana. Remember Cana? Jesus had been there several months ago and had revealed His glory to His family and first followers at the wedding. Why was He going back to this town? What would He do this time? Take a look.

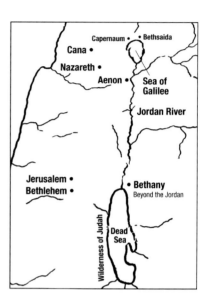

Read: John 4:43-54; Luke 4:14-15. Jot down what you discover in each of the three areas:

What do we know about this royal official?

How many different people did Jesus impact through this miracle?

What do you see as the primary lesson of this passage?

What other questions do you still have?

Outside the Box

As Jesus returns to the district of Galilee, word of His outburst at the temple during the Passover has already sparked the interest of the people. They are waiting with great expectancy for what He will do as He returns home. News must have reached the large city of Capernaum, where it encountered a family suffering deeply as they watched their son slowly dying.

I can only imagine the pain that this royal family experienced as doctor after doctor told them that all their money could not bring their son back to health. There was nothing more they, as doctors, could do; the rest was in the hands of the gods. They had all but lost hope when news about a prophet of the Jews reached their ears. We believe this royal family was Roman; living in the large city of Capernaum working for the government of Rome. We do not know for sure, but we do know they are hurting and at the end of their own ability to help their son. They will try anything. Could this new prophet help their dying child? Put yourself in this family's shoes.

Jesus makes His way back to the city of Cana, possibly to check on the newlyweds. Remember last time He was in Cana, He was attending a wedding. Whose wedding? Some believe it may have been the wedding of one of His family. Remember Mary, His mother, had the inside scoop about the details of the wedding, maybe it was because it was the wedding of one of her daughters. Who knows? But, for whatever reason we can be sure that Jesus returned to Cana because it was God's will. Jesus is very clear about this. Throughout His life, Jesus says time and again that He speaks and moves about, not of His own initiative, but as the Father directs (John 8:28-29). He is living by faith and working off the Father's master plan.

Meanwhile, this royal official makes his way from Capernaum in hopes that Jesus will come with him and heal his son. How does this man know Jesus can heal people? How many people has Jesus healed at this point in His ministry? That's right — none. Yet, this man is desperate. Parents who have an ill child will do anything to help the child. What I don't want you to miss here is the incredible faith of this man. He did not know if Jesus would come back with him to heal his son or even if Jesus was able to heal at all. Yet when Jesus says, *"'You may go. Your son will live'"* (John 4:50), the man believed Jesus and obeyed. What is that? That, my friend, is faith. Faith is taking Jesus at His word, believing Him and then acting in obedience upon what He has said. You see it here in a real-life example, the faith that Jesus so wanted us, His followers, to grasp. This man displayed a faith that pleased God. The result of his faith was not only that his son was physically healed, but also that he and his whole family believed and were saved (John 4:53).

Are you willing to take Jesus at His word, obey what He has said and live it out (2 Cor. 5:7)?

Savior of the World

"They said to the woman, 'We no longer believe just because of what you said; now we have heard for ourselves, and we know that this man really is the Savior of the world.'"

John 4:42

Personal Notes

Day 14   **63**

SEEING GOD

Live It Out

Jesus moved through life in humble submission to the will of the Father, always in obedience to His Dad in heaven. Jesus lived by faith. We know this because without faith it is impossible to please God (Heb. 11:6) and Jesus always pleased the Father (John 8:29). How about you? Are you living by faith or by sight? Find a friend today to discuss what it means to live by faith. Share what you have been learning.

Other Thoughts

Digging Deeper

Hebrews 11:1-6

Genesis 1:1-31

Hebrews 11:7

Genesis 6:11-22

Hebrews 11:8-21

Genesis 12:1-4

Hebrews 11:22

Genesis 50:22-26

Hebrews 11:23-29

Exodus 2:1-14

DAY 15 | Without Faith

Jesus now moves back to the His hometown of Nazareth, the place where he had grown up. Remember what it had been like for Jesus from your study in Psalms 69? Jesus may have suffered here in His youth at the hands of the elders who had constantly discussed what they were going to do with Him and the town drunkards who seemingly made up songs about Him. Now He was returning to teach in their synagogue on the Sabbath. What will happen?

Read: Luke 4:16-30. Jot down what you discover in each of the three areas:

What is this passage telling us about the person of Jesus?

Why the anger in His hometown? (v. 28)

What was their problem? Also see a later visit in Mark 6:1-6.

What other questions do you still have?

Physician

"Jesus said to them, 'Surely you will quote this proverb to me: Physician, heal yourself!'"

Luke 4:23

Personal Notes

Outside the Box

Wow! Did you catch that drastic change in atmosphere? Jesus reads from the Old Testament scroll of Isaiah and the people are riveted on Him. They are listening intently and they are astonished. Look again at verse 22. What is the atmosphere like as Jesus sits down after reading the Word of God and says, *"'Today this scripture is fulfilled in your hearing'"*? The people are all speaking well of Jesus and are somewhat shocked, saying, "Isn't that Joseph the carpenter's son, that kid we thought would never be worth anything?" Now, note the change in atmosphere by Verse 28. Go ahead and read it again. The people are filled with rage and ready to kill Jesus. How do you go from speaking well of someone to being ready to kill him? Something happens between verses 22 and 28 that changes everything. The people went from praising Jesus to wanting to kill Him. What could Jesus have said or done to invoke such a radical change in the people? I think you may need to stop and reread verses 23-27 again before you go on.

Jesus begins by sharing what He can plainly see on their faces, "I know what you want — you want me to do what I did in Capernaum." What had they heard that Jesus had done in Capernaum? It was yesterday's story of the physical healing of the royal officer's son. Jesus could read it on their faces, and maybe they had already begun to say to Him, "'Do here in your own hometown what we have heard you did in Capernaum.'" It is Jesus' response to what they are asking for that will send the crowd through the roof.

Jesus basically says, "Because of your lack of faith, you will not be seeing and tasting what I have to offer. Instead, just like in the days of Elijah the prophet, the heavens will be shut for you. But instead," (and this is what set them off) "I will do what was done in days past; I will heal and cleanse, but not Jews. I will help non-Jews. I will heal people like the woman of Zarephath and cleanse people like Naaman the Syrian captain."

What a slap in the face! But why? Why would Jesus be so tough and speak so sharply to the people from His own hometown? Again, the comparison is to the Old Testament stories of Elijah and Elisha. We also get a hint in Mark 6:4-6. It was because of their unbelief, their lack of faith. Faith is what energizes the work of God in your life and in the lives of those around you. Without faith, God has chosen not to work. He could work apart from our faith and on occasion does, but as a rule, God has chosen to allow us to be part of the process and to trust and obey Him. How is your faith? Do you want to see God move? **Live by faith** and you will see the impossible happen before your very eyes. Think about it.

This root of faith is a huge one. Without it you cannot be pleasing to your Dad in heaven (Heb. 11:6). I challenge you to dig a little deeper into the story of Elijah and Elisha and see faith in action.

Live It Out

Faith is key in your walk as a Christ-follower. The power of God is ignited in you as you willingly choose to live by faith and not by sight. The word "faithful" is often confused with the word loyal or with the concept of loyalty. Yet faithful means to be full of faith. God is looking for faithful men and women, people full of faith — faith in God, not in yourself, your abilities, your government, your ideals or your resources. The object of your faith is key. You will not have faith in Jesus if you do not know Him. The more you know God the more you will trust Him and obey Him; in other words, the more faith you will have in Him. Spend some time today talking to one of your friends about this concept of faith and being faithful.

Other Thoughts

Digging Deeper

Hebrews 11:6 — Memorize it.

Isaiah 61:1-2

1 Kings 17:1-18:1

James 5:16-18

2 Kings 5:1-14

Hebrews 13:12-14

2 Timothy 2:13

Ministry Training and Expanded Outreach: Days 16–25

Sharing in the Multiplication

These next two phases in Jesus' life we have titled Ministry Training and Expanded Outreach. We do this because we see Jesus doing two things here at the same time. As the movement of multiplication grows, Jesus issues His next call:

"'Come, follow me' Jesus said, 'and I will make you fishers of men.'" (Mark 1:17)

It is the third call. It is made to those He has already called: *"Come and see"* and *"Follow Me."* This third call is to come closer to Jesus, to draw near enough so He can now teach you how you can be a part of the process of making disciples. He invites these first followers to join Him in the ministry, to become apprentices in the school of disciple-making and share in the multiplication of the movement.

In this phase of Jesus' ministry you will note that Jesus is now not just modeling things for His followers, but training them to make disciples. He is asking them to come closer and observe more carefully what He has been doing for the last year and a half of the ministry. Thus, Jesus will begin to train His new ministry team. At the same time we see that Jesus' strategy to train His team is an on-the-job training. It is not classroom training, but training as they walk through their day-to-day lives. Because of Jesus' love for those who do not yet know Him, He begins doing outreach activities, or better said, He begins fishing expeditions in which His new disciples will have an opportunity to participate. It is impossible to train someone to fish for men without taking them out fishing. This phase of the movement of multiplication is the training of the ministry team. At the same time, He is having Expanded Outreach. You cannot do the first without doing the second. In order to train His team, He must provide them opportunities to practice what He has been modeling.

This phase in Jesus' ministry will last about nine months. It will include on-the-job training in disciple-making through the first six "Fishing Expeditions" of Jesus. Jesus will continue to do these fishing expeditions as a way of continuing His training with His team. As the movement grows, so do the sizes of the fishing trips. But you will note that the fishing expeditions begin small and gradually gain size and speed. It is an exciting time in the movement as Jesus' fame is mounting and His disciples begin to experience the thrill of calling people to *"Come and see"* and to *"Follow Me."* They believe that Jesus is the **way** to a relationship with the Father. Then they are learning that Jesus is not only the way, but that He is the **truth**. Now He calls them to come closer and learn what it means to have Jesus as the **life**, to become part of a lifestyle of reaching out and calling people. It is an exciting time to be in a movement with as much activity as this one! Come take a look at how Jesus taught His first team how to fish for men.

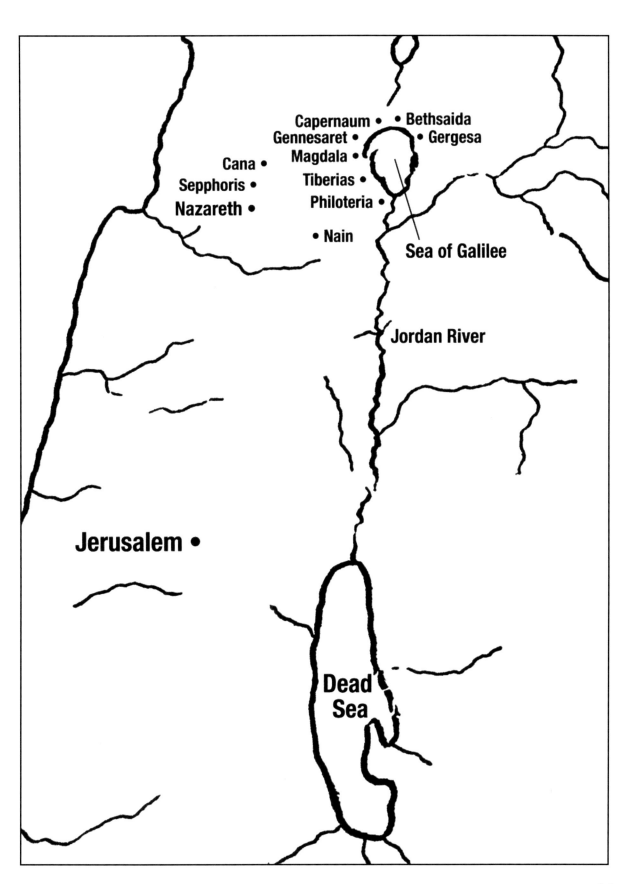

Capernaum •   • Bethsaida
Gennesaret •   • Gergesa
Cana •   Magdala •
Sepphoris •   Tiberias •
Nazareth •   Philoteria •

• Nain

Sea of Galilee

Jordan River

Jerusalem •

Dead
Sea

CHRONOLOGY

Sharing in Multiplication

Jesus goes up to Jerusalem for the Feast of Jews	John 5:1
Jesus heals sick man at Bethesda Pool	John 5:2-15
Jesus before the religious leaders	John 5:16-47
Walk home to Capernaum	Luke 4:31
Jesus casts out demons	Luke 4:33-37; Mark 1:21-28
Jesus goes to Peter's house in Bethsadia	Luke 4:38-39; Mark 1:29-37; Matthew 8:14-17
Jesus makes tour through all Galilee in city synagogues	Mark 1:39; Matthew 4:23
Jesus fills the nets with fish	Luke 5:1-11
Jesus heals the leper	Luke 5:12-13; Mark 1:40-45; Matthew 8:2-4
Jesus heals the paralytic man	Luke 5:17-26; Mark 2:1-12; Matthew 9:1-8
Calling of Levi (Matthew)	Luke 5:27-39; Mark 2:13-22; Matthew 9:9-17
Sabbath Controversy — Jesus, Lord of the Sabbath	Luke 6:1-5; Mark 2:23-28; Matthew 12:1-8
Jesus heals withered hand, large crowds following	Luke 6:6-11; Mark 3:1-6; Matthew 12:9-14

DAY 16 | Jesus on the Move

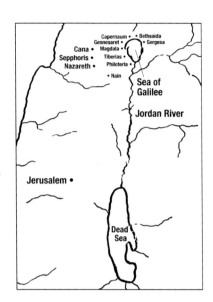

Jesus now moves into a period of transition in the ministry. After preaching in Nazareth in His hometown synagogue and being rejected by the people, Jesus moves (and some believe Jesus also moved His whole family with Him). Where will He go and how will the ministry change? His fame is becoming widespread now and people are coming from all over looking for Him. Jesus, during this time, will make four transitions that we want to note before we look at the training of the His ministry team and the six "Fishing Expeditions." Take a look!

Read: Matthew 4:12-22; Mark 1:14-20; John 3:24.

What is Jesus modeling during this time of transition?

What do we know about Capernaum and Galilee from these passages (and any other passages)?

What do you think are some of Jesus' thoughts?

What other questions do you still have?

A Great Light

"...the people living in darkness have seen a great light; on those living in the land of the shadow of death a light has dawned."

Matthew 4:16

Personal Notes

Outside the Box

After a year and a half of investment in His first followers, Jesus takes some time out to make some significant changes in His life circumstances to prepare Himself and His team for this new season of great harvest. One of the first transitions Jesus makes is a physical move from the small town of Nazareth to the more populated city of Capernaum (Matt. 4:13). Jesus heads off to Capernaum to relocate the ministry to a larger center where there were more people and more business going on. He needed to be closer to the masses he so wanted to reach. If you want to examine why He does this, read the prophesy in the Digging Deeper section (Isa. 9:1-2).

Another transition is one of leadership — like the passing of leadership from John the Baptist to Jesus. John goes to prison as Jesus is moving His home to Capernaum (Matt. 4:12). We will look more fully at this in the next two days as we see Jesus attend the second Passover of His ministry and He takes the platform in front of all Israel as the new leader.

The third transition is a transition in message. Jesus begins to preach, *"'Repent, for the kingdom of heaven is near'"* (Matt. 4:17). We will also be looking more closely at this change in message, but part of the reason for the change is surely because John has gone off the scene and his message had been the same (Matt. 3:2). With John in prison, Jesus picks up this battle cry as well. He is still telling people that He is the Messiah, but He takes over for John and calls Israel to repentance.

The fourth transition is a transition in calling. Jesus issues a new call to His young followers: *"'Come, follow me,' Jesus said, 'and I will make you fishers of men'"* (Matt. 4:19.) People begin to leave their fish nets and families and to follow him. It was a call to come closer and learn to multiply disciples. They were excited and ready for the new challenge. Are you? Maybe it is time to move from being a Christ-follower to being a disciple of Christ. A follower comes and goes as he wants, a disciple has left everything to follow Christ. A disciple has sold-out, he is a Jesus freak, consumed with nothing but Jesus. Jesus has become his consuming thought. A disciple hangs on every word that Jesus says. He is working to *"take captive every thought to make it obedient to Christ"* (2 Cor. 10:5). We will be looking more at this move from Christ-follower to disciple in the coming days and will watch it take place in those early followers as they are challenged to become an active part in the harvesting of disciples.

Live It Out

Transitions in life are really important. Equally important are transitions in ministry. We can learn a lot from studying how Jesus transitioned in His life and ministry. Take some time today to share with a friend what you are learning about Jesus' transitions in His life. Also, do some self-examining and ask yourself where you are in your relationship with Jesus. Are you a Christ follower or a disciple of Christ?

Other Thoughts

Digging Deeper

Matthew 10:37-39

Matthew 16:24-27

Mark 8:34-38

Luke 14:25-35

DAY 17 | To Tell the Truth

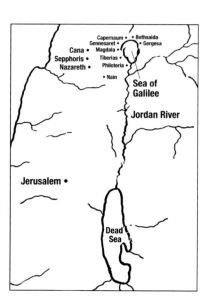

After moving to Capernaum, Jesus makes the long trip down to Jerusalem for the Feast of the Jews. (Some believe this was the second Passover that Jesus attended. Some believe it was the Feast of Tabernacles, thus placing the following two events about 6-7 months later.) Remember what happened last year at the Passover (John 2)? Jesus definitely shook things up then! I wonder what will happen this year. There must have been a buzz about Jesus as people made the journey from all over the world to Jerusalem to celebrate this important Jewish festival. Let's find out what happens.

Read: John 5:1-17.

What does this passage tell us about this sick man?

Why do you think Jesus asked him *"Do you want to get well?"* (v. 6)?

How would you describe this guy to someone else?

What did this miracle stir up in the Jews?

What other questions do you still have?

Outside the Box

Jesus heads south and up to Jerusalem for this Feast of the Jews. Something to keep in mind when reading your Bible is that up does not necessarily mean north, it just means up in elevation. Jerusalem is located on top of a mountain range and is at one of the highest places of elevation in the area. Jesus arrives at the Feast of the Jews and makes His way to a place just outside the wall called Bethesda, close to the Sheep Gate, where there was a multitude of sick people lying around. How many did Jesus heal? One — that's all. A common misconception is that Jesus healed everyone. He did not. He only healed those the Father told Him to heal (John 14:10). Each person was healed for one purpose: to glorify the Father (John 17:4). Jesus' passion in life was to glorify His Father by obeying Him and living a life of faith.

I find this whole story very fascinating, starting with Jesus' rather peculiar question to a man who had been an invalid for 38 years. Jesus asked him, *"'Do you want to get well?'"* (John 5:6). What kind of question is that? Or what about the fact that so many versions of the Bible eliminate or call into question verse 4? Look back and see. Maybe your version of the Bible has it as a footnote or says that many manuscripts do not contain this verse. Wow, that is unusual! I personally believe the verse should be there, because it is interesting that this crazy story of an angel coming down, stirring the water in the pool and healing people would catch John's attention and be included in his gospel.

Most people hold the common view that Jesus was moved with compassion when He saw this needy man. Walking past many others, He listened to His Father's voice and chose to heal this crippled man. This man then became the catalyst for the encounter with the Jews in the following verses. This may be the correct version of what happened.

However, I have a different view, and I believe it has some substance. What if this whole story, about the angel coming and stirring the water was a **lie**, hatched by a man who had been there for 38 years (or someone like him)? What if, as a crusty old con man, he had made up the story and was benefiting from the pains of other people, by gathering them together at the pool to increase the likelihood of receiving donations? Could this be why Jesus asked him such a direct question about if he wanted to get well? After healing this man, there seems to be no repentance of any kind, no gratitude shown and no faith in Jesus expressed. And when he reports that he doesn't know who healed him, we see Jesus tracking him down and telling him, *"'Stop sinning or something worse may happen to you.'"* (John 5:14). Seemingly, the man then goes to the Jews and basically turns in Jesus to the leaders, setting up the confrontation where Jesus so passionately seeks to persuade the leaders of who He is. They then would try even harder to kill Him.

Whichever view you hold, it doesn't change the flow of the story. Either this man was a needy person on whom Jesus had compassion or a hard man that seemingly did not respond with faith or gratitude and then turns Jesus in to the Jews. You find this event setting up the opportunity to preach the truth in the temple area, much like what Peter experienced in Acts 3. The Father's definite plan was the healing of this man for a truth encounter with the religious leaders during the Jews' festival.

The Truth

"Jesus answered, 'I am the way and the truth and the life. No one comes to the Father except through me.'"

John 14:6

Personal Notes

SEEING GOD

Live It Out

Perhaps I see this story differently than most, but all my life I have struggled to tell the truth, and I can see in this man a similar trait. No gratitude, no expressed faith and a tendency to keep on sinning. Maybe you can identify with my struggle. I am so glad that when Jesus saved me, He put His truth in me and His truth set me free. Lying is a tough thing to talk about with another person. It is at our core and is something we find hard to admit to and talk about. I am going to ask you to do a hard thing today and share with a friend about your struggle to tell the truth. If you do not feel you have a struggle in this area, maybe you can share some secrets you have discovered to being a truth-teller. Regardless of where you are at, have a discussion with some friends today about lying and telling the truth.

Other Thoughts

Digging Deeper

Proverbs 6:17

Jeremiah 17:21-22

John 8:41-47

Colossians 3:9

Titus 1:2

1 John 2:3-6

DAY 18 | Jesus, the Truth-Teller

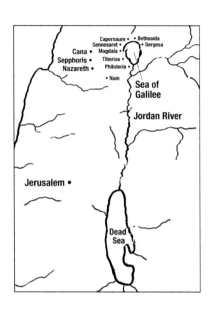

This is a big day for Jesus! Today he will appear before the religious leaders in Jerusalem. He is being brought up on two very serious charges. **Charge #1:** Jesus broke Sabbath by healing a man and then telling him to carry his mat (do work). **Charge #2:** Jesus was claiming that God was His real Father and that He and God the Father were equals. Wow! I hope you can't wait for the declaration of truth that is coming your way today.

Read: John 5:16-47.

What was the primary message of Jesus in this passage (v. 18)?

There are several witnesses that Jesus calls forward to testify on His behalf. Find them and write down the truth they tell about who Jesus is.

What does this discourse by Jesus tell us about His character?

What other questions do you still have?

Son of God

"'I tell you the truth, a time is coming and has now come when the dead will hear the voice of the Son of God and those who hear will live.'"

John 5:25

Personal Notes

Outside the Box

There has never been and never will be a more powerful declaration of the person of Jesus Christ than what we see in this passage. Here we have Jesus Christ Himself, addressing the religious and political leaders of His day in an all-out defense of who He is. Like a masterful lawyer, Jesus works His way through point by point, witness by witness, to the logical conclusion that He really is equal with God. He argues that it is a fact and not blasphemous at all. Here is Jesus, fully God, and yet standing before them fully man. He is the God and Man, God made in flesh, God come to live as His creations do and show us how to live in complete dependence on the Father.

How did you do with the five witnesses? Let's take a brief look at each one.

Witness #1: Jesus Himself (John 5:19-31). Jesus says that He is loved by the Father (v. 20), has an ongoing intimate relationship with Him, was given authority by the Father to execute judgment and is willing to submit to the Father and do only His will (vs. 19, 30). He also says that He is equal with God (v. 23).

Witness #2: John the Baptist (John 5:33,35). John gave testimony of who Jesus was, back at the Jordan River (John 1:19-34). John testified that Jesus was the Messiah, the Lamb of God, who came to take away the sins of the world. Unfortunately, John is now rotting in prison, his light hidden from the people.

Witness #3: Jesus' Own Works (John 5:36). Jesus says that greater than the testimony of the prophet John is Jesus' works that God has given Him to do. The miracles of transformed lives all around Him bear witness of His authenticity, like the man who was sick for 38 years before Jesus healed him.

Witness #4: The Father Himself (John 5:37,38). Jesus now calls God the Father to witness about His true self. But when did the Father testify about Jesus? Go back to the river again (Matt. 3:16-17). The Father opened the heavens and said, *"'This is my Son, whom I love; with him I am well pleased.'"*

Witness #5: The Scripture (John 5:39-47). Jesus tells them, *"'But do not think I will accuse you before the Father. Your accuser is Moses, on whom your hopes are set. If you believed Moses, you would believe me, for he wrote about me'"* (John 5:45-46). Wow! But what does He mean, that Moses wrote about Him? I have read the first five books of the Bible (those that Moses wrote) and I have never seen anything about Jesus there. Unfortunately, our generation has long lost the fact that the Bible, the whole Bible, is really all about Jesus, and not about us. In our individualistic society we have been taught to read and study the Bible looking for ourselves. What does it say about me? What am I suppose to do? What does God want from me? These are all good questions, but not the real point of the Bible. From cover to cover, the Bible points to Jesus. It is the same with history, we tend to interpret history in terms of ourselves and not Jesus. We are self-centered, instead of Christ-centered. Really, all of history is simply His story (Jesus' Story).

Live It Out

My challenge to you is to read the Word of God, not looking for you, but looking for **Him.** I guarantee a life change. Spend some time today sharing who Jesus is with a friend — not who you think Jesus is but who Jesus says He is. In John 5, the man Jesus tells us that He is God and gives proof of that truth. Discuss Jesus with a friend who does not know Him yet. Use John 5 as your source of discussion. Ask them simply to read it and react to what Jesus says about Himself. You will have to come to the conclusion that either Jesus was mentally ill and self-deceived, a complete nut case, or that He was telling the truth and He was God in an earthly body. After allowing your friend to read this passage and respond, simply ask him/her what they will do with Jesus. Be brave! Be courageous! You will simply be asking someone to read what Jesus said about Himself. You don't have to hardly say a thing. Don't even feel like you need to defend Jesus — He does a much better job than we could ever do. Go ahead and find that friend.

Other Thoughts

Digging Deeper

Deuteronomy 18:15-19

Psalms 119:160

John 1:14

John 8:32

John 14:6

Hebrews 6:18

1 John 1:8-10

1 John 2:4-6

SEEING GOD

DAY 19 | Fishers of Men

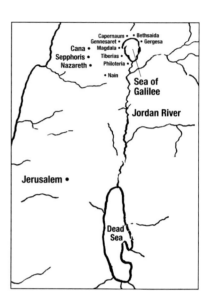

Jesus leaves Jerusalem and makes His way back up north to His new home in Capernaum. He most likely heads over to the shores of the Sea of Galilee to meet up with some of His early followers, who had returned home as well to their parents, wives and families. He arrives early in the morning, just as the sun breaks over the horizon. These fishermen have just come off of a long night of fishing and are hard at work washing and mending their nets. What will Jesus say to them? Will they be excited to see Him?

Read: Matthew 4:18-22; Mark 1:16-20.

Who is Jesus calling? Was this His first encounter with these disciples?

What is Jesus modeling for us in how He called these disciples?

When the disciples hear this call to *"'follow me and I will make you fishers of men,'"* what questions do you think are going through their minds?

What other questions do you still have?

Outside the Box

Let me begin by saying that many people have been confused by the life of Jesus because they have not taken time to study it chronologically, as you are. If you just read Matthew or just read Mark you would see how one might be confused. Both authors appear to have Jesus coming out of the desert in Matthew 4 and Mark 1 and moving right into Capernaum and making the call to become fishers of men. You would not understand that Jesus had already invested over a year and a half in these guys before this call. This is a very significant point. There is almost a year lapse in time between Matthew 4:11 and Matthew 4:12 and between Mark 1:13 and Mark 1:14. But both authors help us by giving us the reference point of John the Baptist going to prison (the latter verse in each pair). I think this is one of the reasons the Holy Spirit prompted the Apostle John to write a fourth gospel. There was much confusion in the early church as to the process of disciple making, and John really helps us see that, although it is not a period of major growth in the ministry, Jesus' earlier investment in His disciples set the stage for the ministry and multiplication movement that we are about to see.

Can you see that before Jesus issued this call to become a "fisher of men," He had already invested more than a year and a half of His life in these early followers? He had not just shared with them the gospel of the kingdom of God, but He had shared His very life with them as well (John 3:22). This call to follow closer comes on the heels of a huge investment of time, energy and life on Jesus' part in these men. He spent all that time modeling for them the disciple-making process and now He calls them to join Him in it. That is why, when Jesus comes walking by, these guys throw down their nets and follow Him. Jesus was not some unknown person to them, but their Messiah and trusted friend. These were not a bunch of naive fisherman, but men with businesses and families. This is not some kind of romantic scene of Jesus walking by the sea of Galilee and saying *"Come, follow me, and I will make you fishers of men!"* where these guys throw down their nets and go running after Him. Jesus had a deep relationship with these guys and it is obvious they had made plans to follow Him and were simply waiting for Him to come and call them. It is something they must have talked about much during the last couple years together. Peter must have talked it over with his wife and mother-in-law. John and James must have talked it over with their father and mother. Notice that their father doesn't run after them or call them back. He lets them go, and we will find out that Zebedee's family is made up of believers, strong supporters of the ministry and key partners in the movement.

Peter and Andrew were from a smaller fishing town just east of the big city of Capernaum (John 1:44). James and John must have lived nearby because their father Zebedee had many hired servants and was in some sort of business partnership with Peter (Luke 5:10). Notice what these four left behind to follow Jesus. Yes, it is true to follow Jesus more closely you must leave some things behind. Even good things. But nonetheless, you must leave them behind if you are to truly follow Jesus and His Father's will. Peter left behind his business, and we will find out later that he also left his family behind. James and John left behind their father and their part in the business to follow after Jesus. You will be discovering as we go along what else Jesus calls these guys, and us, to leave behind so that the Father can use us. What do you need to leave behind?

Rabbi

"Turning around, Jesus saw them following and asked, 'What do you want?' They said, 'Rabbi '(which means Teacher), 'where are you staying?'"

John 1:38

Personal Notes

SEEING GOD

Live It Out

I want to repeat what I said earlier. Jesus invested more than a year and a half of His life in these early followers. He did not just share with them the gospel of the kingdom of God, but He shared His very life with them as well. Paul, always following the example of Jesus (1 Cor. 11:1), shares the same sentiment with his dear friends in the town of Thessalonica. Take a look at 1 Thessalonians 2:8. Let it sink in deep. God desires that you impart life and not just the message of the gospel. Spend some time discussing with the people you are investing your life in about how they can invest in others as well. Challenge them today with the life of Jesus and follow His lead. Who are you investing your life in?

Other Thoughts

Digging Deeper

Matthew 28:18-20

Luke 14:25-35

1 Corinthians 4:16

1 Thessalonians 2:8

2 Timothy 2:2

DAY 20 | Fishing Expedition One

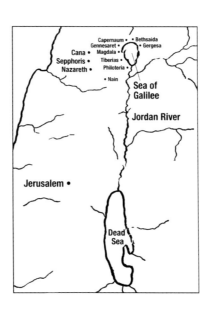

Jesus is now ready to begin what will be another year and a half of fishing expeditions with His disciples. We will be looking at the first six expeditions. These are the first six outreach events that Jesus does in order to train His young ministry team to reach the masses with the Good News that He is the Messiah. There is a progression to these fishing trips, a good pattern for us to follow, and much to learn about fishing for men. Read the story from the three different points of view, or better yet, print them out and try to piece the event together chronologically. Jump right in and learn to fish Jesus-style.

Read: Luke 4:31-37; Mark 1:21-28. Jot down what you discover in each of the these areas:

Where is Jesus fishing?

Who is Jesus fishing for?

What is Jesus modeling about fishing for men in a religious setting?

How is Jesus fishing?

What other questions do you still have?

The Holy One of God

"'Ha! What do you want with us, Jesus of Nazareth? Have you come to destroy us? I know who you are — the Holy One of God!'"

Luke 4:34

Personal Notes

Outside the Box

Jesus begins these fishing expeditions in the religious center of His day, the Jewish synagogue. After issuing the call to follow closer so that He could teach them to fish for men, Jesus takes His new disciples back into Capernaum and decides the first fishing expedition will be at the synagogue. The event takes place on a Saturday, the Sabbath. Jesus most likely did some training on how to fish for men before the event, maybe at a home.

Jesus comes in ready, ready to model for His team how to fish for men and ready to share with the masses in this large synagogue at Capernaum who He is. Jesus enters and begins to teach. Remember His strategy of sharing with the religious lost? Is it the same? He goes straight to the Torah, the books of Moses, the first five in the Bible, and shares with them who He is (Luke 24:27). Remember, Jesus is now not only sharing who He is, but also preaching that the time has come to repent and believe the Good News, because the kingdom of God is at hand. While He is teaching, the crowd is filled with amazement. What was so amazing about what Jesus said and did? First, they were amazed that He taught with authority, like He really believed what He was saying, in comparison to the scribes who must have been teaching half-heartedly (Mark 1:22). Second, they were amazed at this new teaching, or new doctrine (Mark 1:27). And lastly, they were amazed that Jesus was in command of the evil spirit in this man.

How many demons has Jesus cast out so far? That's right — none! More than a year and a half of ministry and this is the first demon that Jesus has cast out. Jesus does this major miracle in the synagogue to capture the attention of the people to His message. Something really cool to notice as you keep your eyes open to the declaration of Jesus' deity and humanity is what this demon calls out about Jesus. Take a look back at Mark 1:24. Cool, huh? The demon jeers at him *"Jesus of Nazareth"* and *"the Holy One of God."* There is no doubt in this old demon's mind who Jesus is. The *"Jesus of Nazareth"* illustrates how fully human Jesus was, while *"Holy One of God"* shows that even the demon knows that Jesus was sent from God Almighty. The demon is responding, most likely, to what Jesus has been teaching. Jesus has just been saying that He has come from God and that He is equal to God and that He is God in human form, raised in Nazareth with a real family.

Well, let's evaluate the success of this first fishing expedition. This allows me to challenge you to consider how you evaluate your fishing expeditions. I like to ask three questions to evaluate these types of events. **Question #1:** Were there non-believers at the event? **Question #2:** Was Jesus presented clearly in a culturally relevant way as the Messiah or the Savior of the world? **Question #3:** Did anyone believe the message and put their faith in Jesus for salvation or move closer to accepting His claims to be the Messiah? Take a moment and evaluate this first expedition. How did Jesus and His team do?

Live It Out

I am going to ask you to start praying about an expedition of your own in the next week — something simple, not a concert with 50,000 people, but something small. What might you do? Who can you invite to join to help you in this fishing expedition? Get together with a few friends and start thinking and praying for those around you who do not know that Jesus is the Savior of the world. Start thinking of something you can do to present the claims of Jesus in a culturally relevant way. Your assignment today is to begin to form a group of friends whom you disciple, and start to think about what you could do. Meanwhile, keep studying how Jesus conducted His fishing expeditions and each day you will learn more in the process. But get started. Pray about whom to invite. Jot down their names:

Other Thoughts

Digging Deeper

Mark 5:30

Mark 6:5-6

Luke 5:17

Luke 6:19

Luke 24:27,32,44

Philippians 2:9-11

Hebrews 1:1-3

DAY 21 | Fishing Expedition Two

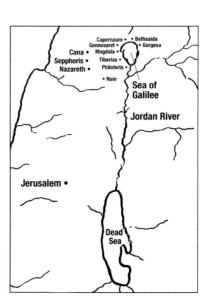

We are in the process of looking at the first six fishing expeditions of Jesus. We are doing this for two reasons. Do you remember what they are? His aim was both to train the ministry team and to reach the masses. Although yesterday's expedition was well executed, today's fishing expedition may surprise you. When we left yesterday, Jesus had healed a demon-possessed man of an evil spirit and, immediately, news about Jesus spread into all the surrounding district of Galilee (Mark 1:28). Jesus leaves the synagogue in Capernaum and heads to Peter's house. Yes, Peter owned a house and he was even married. Check it out.

Read: Luke 4:38-44; Matthew 8:14-17; Mark 1:29-39. Jot down what you discover in each of the these areas:

Where is Jesus fishing?

Who is Jesus fishing for?

What is Jesus modeling about fishing for men in a house setting?

How is Jesus fishing?

What other questions do you still have?

Outside the Box

Today, we are at Peter's home for a very different kind of fishing expedition — a home outreach, beginning in the evening after sunset. Because of the news of what had happened in the synagogue in Capernaum, word of Jesus' authority, power and message had carried to the surrounding area and people came to bring their sick and demon-possessed. The first outreach was in a synagogue and the second in a disciple's home, two very different places to reach people with the Good News about Jesus. Another huge difference in this outreach event was that it was a spontaneous event that probably lasted long into the night, judging by the amount of people who showed up. Notice once again that Jesus does not heal everyone or cast out every evil spirit (Mark 1:34).

Once again, let me remind you that although Jesus may have wanted to heal everyone He came in contact with, He only healed those the Father allowed Him to. He always said and did what the Father told Him to. I think many times Jesus did not heal people because the Father was more glorified in the sickness than in the healing of the person. I know this is a tough truth to wrestle with, especially when you are face-to-face with a parent or someone you love who has cancer or some deadly disease. Yet, we must understand, as Jesus did, that it is about bringing glory to the Father and not about earthly, temporal comfort. Every person Jesus healed eventually died.

Another thing I do not want you to miss is what happens the morning after this great night of ministry. Look back and check it out. What does Jesus do and when does He do it (Mark 1:35)? Jesus, after a long night of ministry, gets up before dawn and slips out of the house to get alone with His Father. Wow! How cool is that? A quiet time with His Father was not just a once-in-awhile thing for Jesus. He modeled a lifestyle of getting alone with His Father, to hear His voice, to find out the next steps in life and ministry and just to commune with Him (Luke 5:16). Do you have this passion in you to know God as Father and commune with Him? Notice that after meeting with His Dad, Jesus' disciples come looking for Him. That is because they had already gotten excited about these fishing expeditions and had gone ahead and seemingly planned one on their own (or at least Peter did). "Come back, Jesus," they called to Him. "Everyone is looking for you and we need you to go!"

It sounds a lot like a few events I have tried to organize. I did all the planning and, at the last moment, asked Jesus to show up. And he would say, "Not now, my son. Maybe next time you should talk with the Father beforehand." Jesus, in this case, shocks them all by telling them no because they needed to leave to preach in the next towns. I can only imagine the looks on their faces. How did Jesus know it was time to move on? Remember, He had just spent the early hours with His Father, getting the next steps. So, acting in obedience, Jesus does the will of God and not the will of men. As you plan your event, do so with the Father and not without Him. Ask for His guidance from the beginning. He so wants to be included in every part of your life and not be an add-on in the end.

Prayer

"Very early in the morning, while it was still dark, Jesus got up, left the house and went off to a solitary place, where he prayed."

Mark 1:35

Personal Notes

SEEING GOD

Live It Out

Jesus loved getting away to be with His Dad, to hear His voice, to get His next steps and to commune with Him. How about you? Do you have this Jesus lifestyle of making time to be with your Father? This is such an important part of your walk with Christ. Your discussion today with your disciples is about having a lifestyle of meeting with God. Share honestly about how hard this is in the busy world in which you find yourself. Satan will do everything he can to keep you from spending time with your Dad. Don't let him win.

It is time to start thinking about a date for your fishing expedition, if you have not already. You must immerse yourself in prayer. Ask the Father to identify the people you are to reach out to and who will join the fishing team. Pray for them and involve them in planning the expedition.

Other Thoughts

Digging Deeper

Mark 1:35

Luke 3:21-22

Luke 5:16

Luke 6:12

Luke 10:21-22

Luke 11:1-13

Luke 21:37

Luke 22:39-46

John 17:1-26

Hebrews 5:7

DAY 22 | Fishing Expedition Three

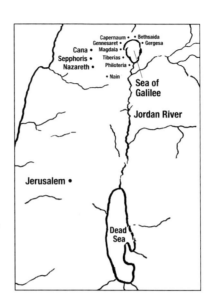

Okay, so far we have Jesus fishing at the synagogue and at the disciple Peter's house. Where will He go next? One outreach was well planned, the other spontaneous. What kind of event will follow? When we left Jesus yesterday, under the direction of His Father, He had departed with His disciples (or at least most of them) for the surrounding villages to train His young team and go fishing for men. Fishing in the marketplace is where we will find the Master today. Check it out.

Read: Luke 5:1-11.

Where is Jesus fishing?

What are some of the various emotions Jesus' disciples were feeling?

Verse 8 says that *"When Simon Peter saw this, he fell down at Jesus' knees ..."* **What was** *"this"*?

What other questions do you still have?

Master

"Simon answered, 'Master, we've worked hard all night and haven't caught anything. But because you say so, I will let down the nets.'"
Luke 5:5

Personal Notes

Outside the Box

Jesus begins to make His way around the Sea of Galilee, more of a large lake than an actual sea. He continues to provide His young team on-the-job training fishers of men. Jesus and His disciples arrive in the early morning on the shores of the port town of Gennesaret, on the western banks of the Sea of Galilee, just southwest of Capernaum. The people begin to arrive as well to buy the fish for the day. Remember that there were no refrigerators in that time and people bought their food fresh each day at the water's edge as the fishermen arrived from a full night of fishing. Jesus takes advantage of the opportunity and begins the next training session, an "open air" outreach event. Notice Jesus' strategy — He doesn't try to assemble a huge number of people. He just goes where the people are. He knew there would be a crowd of people gathered to buy fish in the morning. He uses an already existing event and turns it into an opportunity to do some of His own fishing and training with His disciples.

As Jesus is teaching the crowd, the people start to press in on Him to touch Him. As the people press in on Him, He continues to back up and ends up knee-deep in water and still moving out. Jesus realizes that He needs some help and begins to look around. Who of all people does He see? It's Peter. Now wait a minute — you would've thought Peter was already with Jesus, but evidently not. Peter must have gone back to fishing for fish at some point. Maybe Peter never left with the group, after Jesus shut down His outreach event in His hometown that he had planned. Maybe Peter was struggling with leaving everything to follow after Jesus. After all, he had a wife, maybe children, a mother-in-law, a house and a business. Peter was older in life and definitely had accumulated more things that he would have to give up. We gain insight into this as the outreach unfolds.

After getting in Peter's boat, the two of them head a little ways out as Jesus continues to teach the people. I imagine He was teaching something like, "I am Jesus of Nazareth. I am fully human and yet I am the Messiah and fully God. If I wanted to, I could tell this fishermen to put down his nets and he would pull in so many fish that his boat couldn't hold them all. In fact, I think I will do that. What do you think, Father?" Remember, the people had come to buy fish this morning and it seems that there was nothing to buy as we read Peter's response, "We've worked hard and been out here all night, but haven't caught anything!" Peter must have been thinking, "Hey, I'm the fisherman here and you're a carpenter, Jesus. If I fished all night and didn't catch anything, so there are probably no fish to be caught." However, Peter obeys and pushes a little further out and drops his nets — maybe to prove to Jesus that he, Peter, knows what he is talking about. Can you imagine the scene on the beach as everyone watches in amazement as Peter drops his nets in daylight and fish start jumping everywhere? People must have certainly started screaming, "I can't believe it — Jesus really must be the Messiah." Meanwhile, on the boat, Peter falls at Jesus' knees (Luke 5:8). Yes, His knees, because there were so many fish in the boat that they were both knee-deep in fish. Peter cries out, *"Go away from me, Lord; I am a sinful man!"* (v. 8). Jesus responds by telling Peter not to be afraid but to become a fisher of men from now on. Jesus gives Peter a second chance, and Peter takes it and leaves behind everything to follow Jesus. I wonder what happened to all the fish they caught and left behind (Luke 5:11)? Could it be that Jesus was showing Peter that He is fully capable of meeting all his family's needs? Could this miracle be for Peter — that Jesus truly is Jehovah-Jireh (The Great Provider)?

Live It Out

What does it mean to leave everything to follow Jesus? Later, in John 21, after Jesus rises from the dead, we see Peter back fishing. This will be the last time. Jesus meets him again and repeats this same miracle to remind Peter that He is Lord. He can take care of providing for you and your family. I think Peter was struggling with believing that Jesus was Lord of all. Jesus spoke to Him in terms Peter could understand, showing Peter that He was capable of doing what Peter could not. He could catch fish when Peter was unable to and He was more than able to provide for him and anyone else if he would only step out in faith and believe. Peter took a step of faith this day that changed his life. Find a friend today and talk about what keeps people from leaving everything to follow after Jesus.

With your small group of friends, continue praying and planning your fishing expedition. Nail down a date and a place to go fishing. Remember, you can go fishing for men in the market place, in a home or at a church. The key is not where but that you actually enter the harvest field and start working. This weekend could be the perfect time. You do not need a lot of preparation time. This is not the Big Event, but a small first step.

Other Thoughts

Digging Deeper

What does it mean when it says they left everything to follow Jesus (Luke 5:11)?
Matthew 10:37-39

Matthew 13:44-46

Matthew 16:24-27

Luke 14:25-35

Philippians 3:7-11

Hebrews 11:26

DAY 23 | Fishing Expedition Four

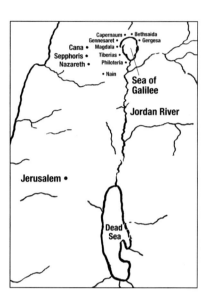

As Jesus moves throughout the Galilee of the Gentiles, sharing who He is, He comes across a man covered from head to toe with a fatal disease. What will happen and how will this lead to a teaching experience and a fishing expedition for His team? Let's dig right in.

Read: Luke 5:12-16; Matthew 8:2-4; Mark 1:40-45.

Where is Jesus fishing?

Who is Jesus fishing for?

What is Jesus modeling about fishing for men in a city?

How is Jesus fishing?

What other questions do you still have?

Outside the Box

As Jesus makes His way from city to city and from town to town he encounters a little bit of everything. In one of the cities He meets a man covered with leprosy. I wonder who Luke heard this story from? Maybe it was the man who was healed, who was then active in the church. Who knows? What we do know is that whoever told Luke was an eyewitness to the event (Luke 1:2).

In the Old Testament, in Leviticus 13:1-59, God gives the official test for leprosy. It is a very detailed and long process to determine if someone has leprosy. Leprosy was a very contagious disease, and the priests, who were the keepers of the public health of the community, had the responsibility to protect the people from the spread of this disease. God gave them very specific things they had to do and observations they had to make when confronted by the reality of this deadly disease. This man was covered with leprosy and had been ostracized from his people because of the disease. The people were deathly afraid of any kind of contact with lepers, so much so, that they made leper colonies live outside the city to keep all the people with this disease together and away from the healthy people. They also made the leprous people yell out "Unclean" whenever anyone would approach them. Can you imagine this kind of existence?

It is interesting to note that Luke says that this man approaches Jesus while He was in the city and doesn't record that he cried out "Unclean." Why not? How did this leper make it into the city? However it happened, he must have made it past the city fathers at the front gate. He is here in front of Jesus with his face in the dirt begging for a touch from the Master. Jesus, moved with compassion, and unafraid of this man's leprosy, extends His hand and touches him. Can you imagine the look on the disciples' faces? They must have been freaked out. What is Jesus doing, reaching out to a leper? Doesn't he know if He touches this guy He will get his leprosy? What a lesson to His young followers! Don't miss it. Jesus loved the outcast, the unlovely, the socially rejected and fished for them as well. This is not the only leper Jesus heals. In fact, I, Mark Edwards, was a leper, spiritually speaking, spotted and stained with sin, when Jesus found me, reached out to me and saved me from sin's deadly disease of self centeredness that covered me. How I praise Him for the day He saved a sin-covered kid from the inner city of Chicago.

Jesus embraces this leper and removes his leprosy at once from him. He heals him on the spot and orders the healed man to tell no one, but to go and show himself as clean to the priest. Meanwhile, Jesus slips away to spend some time with His Dad and ask for direction and the next steps in His ministry (Luke 5:16). This was His habit, His way of life, His lifestyle. Jesus modeled a lifestyle of meeting with the Father, listening to His voice and obeying Him in everything.

Lord

"A man with leprosy came and knelt before him and said, 'Lord, if you are willing, you can make me clean.'"

Matthew 8:2

Personal Notes

SEEING GOD

Live It Out

Think about this for a minute: Who are the lepers in your life? Who are the people in your life that you treat like lepers? We all know a group of people that are outcasts. We avoid them like the plague of leprosy. Go ahead — take a moment and identify the group. God calls you to reach out and fish for lepers. Jesus modeled for you how to do it. You have to reach out and touch them. Maybe God would have you do your fishing expedition to a group of lepers.

Now think about this. You are a leper for some other person. That's right. As good looking, as popular and as great a person as you think you are, you are a leper to someone else. We were all lepers at one time to God, yet He loved us, touched us and paid the ultimate sacrifice to make us clean. He paid with the life of His only Son — Jesus. How is your fishing expedition coming? Keep moving forward. Spend some time praying with and talking to your friends as you finalize the plans.

Other Thoughts

Digging Deeper

Why did Jesus order the man to go show himself to the priest of his town?
Leviticus 13:1-6

Leviticus 13:45-52

What sacrifices was the man to make after being made well?
Leviticus 14:1-32

2 Kings 5:1-14

Luke 17:11-21

DAY 24 | Fishing Expedition Five

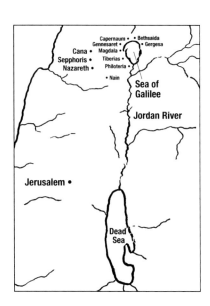

After this last fishing expedition, the movement is snowballing. Did you catch how the movement of multiplication is beginning to get out of control? Peter notes that during this time in the ministry, the leper *"went out and began to talk freely, spreading the news. As a result, Jesus could no longer enter a town openly but stayed outside in lonely place. Yet the people still come to him from everywhere"* (Mark 1:45). From the eyewitnesses that he interviewed, Luke notes: *"Yet the news about him spread all the more, so that crowds of people came to hear him and to be healed of their sicknesses"* (Luke 5:15). What will happen next?

Read: Luke 5:17-26; Matthew 9:1-8; Mark 2:1-13.

Where is Jesus fishing? What is happening here in this passage?

What problems are presented in the text?

Luke 5:20 and Mark 2:5 tells us Jesus *"saw their faith."* What does this tell us about faith?

What lessons were the disciples learning as they watched this event unfold?

What other questions do you still have?

Son of Man

"But that you may
know that the Son of
Man has authority on
earth to forgive sins…"

Mark 2:10

Personal Notes

Outside the Box

This fishing expedition is really a result of the last one. When Jesus healed the leper He told him to tell no one but to go and show himself to the priest? I think the healing of the man with leprosy was, in fact, Jesus' creative invitation to the religious leaders to today's fishing expedition in Capernaum.

On this occasion, Jesus sets up shop for a expedition to the religious leaders. Notice the people who were in this packed house (Luke 5:17). There were Pharisees and teachers of the law from every village of Galilee and Judea and from Jerusalem. Wow! What a gathering! Having attracted a crowd by cleansing a leper, this was the first time that kind of miracle had happened in a long while. Only God could have done that, right? I think Jesus invited these leaders to continue a discussion that He had with them in Jerusalem a few months back. Remember when they had seen Him last? It was at the Passover, and they had accused Him of saying that He was God's Son and claiming to be equal with God Himself (John 5:18). Maybe they had come ready for a fight, ready to throw Jesus a curve ball. Or maybe they came with honest questions? The discussion must have centered around Jesus being God and having the same power as God. What power did God alone have? Did you catch it? God alone could forgive sins (Luke 5:21). Yeah, Jesus, you can't forgive sins, can you?

Some of the religious leaders seemed dead set on proving that Jesus was not God. But they had their hopes crushed as the Father sent four incredible friends, who would not be denied nor would they give up. Instead, they got creative in doing whatever it took to get their friend to Jesus. Do you have any friends like that? Do you love anyone enough to do whatever it takes to get him/her to Jesus? I am not sure how this paralyzed man got four superhero friends who would stop at nothing to get their friend to Jesus. I am also not sure who your superhero friend was that brought you to Jesus, but no one comes to Jesus alone. We all need a friend to call us to *"Come and see."* Who do you love enough to tell them that Jesus is the way to God, the only way (John 14:6)?

Notice how they leave this outreach event (Luke 5:26). Wow! That's right, all of them — the people, the friends, the man and the religious leaders — struck with amazement and glorifying God. The ministry is taking a turn. What will happen next?

Live It Out

Take a few moments and thank God for the person who shared with you the Good News that Jesus is the Messiah. Thank God for giving you a friend that loved you enough that they were willing to take a risk and bring you to Jesus.

Now think of someone you know who needs his/her sins forgiven. Jot their name down: _____. Remember, your friend is spiritually paralyzed. How can you get your friend to Jesus? Spend some time praying and finalizing your fishing expedition plans. It is time to act. Pick one of the fishing expeditions of Jesus and follow His example. Reach out with God's love to those around you who are spiritual lepers and paralytics.

Other Thoughts

SEEING
GOD

Digging Deeper

Nehemiah 9:17

Psalms 130:3-4

Isaiah 43:25

Matthew 26:28

Luke 24:47

Acts 10:43

Ephesians 1:7

Hebrews 9:21-22

DAY 25 | Fishing Expedition Six

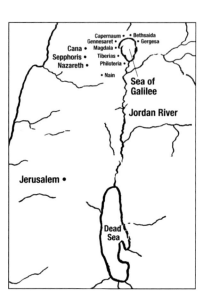

The sixth fishing expedition is amazing and, honestly, a bit astonishing to me. There is this guy living in Capernaum — he is well off, well-dressed, has it all. He is, in fact, the son of the powerful Alphaeus and commissioned, trusted and protected by Rome to collect taxes from the people of Israel. He may have been following Jesus from afar and weighing carefully the call to leave everything and follow. But there is so much to leave — the house, the money, the job, the lifestyle. If he could only know for certain that Jesus could give him what he most wants. Let's see what he discovers.

Read: Luke 5:27-39; Matthew 9:9-17; Mark 2:14-22.

Where is Jesus fishing?

What do we know about tax collectors?

How do you visualize this banquet?

What were Jesus' disciples learning?

What other questions do you still have?

Outside the Box

Once again, this Fishing Expedition is closely tied to the one we just saw yesterday. It would not surprise me to discover that Matthew was one of the people who had his face pressed up against the window as Jesus confronted the unbelief of the religious crowd. I think maybe Matthew heard Jesus say something that day that changed everything for him. You see, Matthew didn't really need anything. He had everything the world of his day had to offer. He probably had a large house. Matthew had the clothes, the money, the house, the horse, the deluxe chariot — everything anyone could possibly want. Yet, there was one thing he did not possess. It is the thing that every wealthy person in the world who does not have Jesus seeks. He did not have forgiveness of sins. As he pressed his ear that day against the window, he heard and saw Jesus forgive sins and prove it with a supernatural miracle.

Jesus begins walking the streets of Capernaum and recognizes Matthew and says, *"Follow Me!"* No sweeter words were ever heard by the hated tax collector. He was a traitor to his own people, a sellout to the enemy — Rome. He was despised and rejected and his only friends were other tax collectors and sinners. Wow! What an act of love, what an extension of grace, what a risk of reputation. Jesus would get branded from this event and His time in Matthew's house. Those who hated Jesus used this opportunity to defame Him and even started a saying about Him. It is found a few chapters later in Matthew 11:19 and also in Luke 7:34. They called Jesus *"a glutton and a drunkard, a friend of tax collectors and 'sinners.'"* What they meant as a slam, Jesus wore as a badge.

How about you? Is anyone calling you a friend of sinners? Or do you stay so far away from the tax collectors and sinners in your life for fear that they might tarnish your squeaky-clean reputation? Be careful whose reputation you are guarding. Jesus loved being known as a friend of sinners. That is why He can be your friend and mine. He humbled Himself taking on the form of a human. I can't even fathom the depth of humility and how low Jesus stooped to come to this sin-sick earth and save a bunch of sinners and tax collectors. Oh, if only sinners would see enough of Jesus in me to call me their friend — not because I partake in their sin, but because I love them and embrace them despite their sin. Remember that even though Jesus hung out with the sinners of His day, He never fell into their sins (Heb. 4:15). Be careful that you bring Jesus to the sinners of this world and they don't draw you into their sins. Be wise, stay closely connected to Jesus and depend on Him for wisdom and discernment as you reach out to a lost and dying world.

Live It Out

Matthew came to Jesus and then right away threw a party for Him. Be ready after your fishing expedition for one of the people who comes to Jesus to be pumped to share Jesus with his/her family or friends. They may even want your help. How exciting! Be ready to follow up with those who will come to Jesus. Don't blow this opportunity. You will never know what it feels like to fish for men until you do it. It is a waste of time to talk about fishing for men and not actually do it. Don't be scared — be strong and courageous and call people to *"Come and see,"* to check out Jesus. This is your chance to see God's power in action as you step out on faith and share the Good News. Spend some time praying together for your follow-up with those who will believe. Remember the fields are ready for the harvest (John 4:35). Throw out the net and experience the thrill of catching men for Jesus.

Teacher

"When the Pharisees saw this, they asked his disciples, 'Why does your teacher eat with tax collectors and 'sinners'?'"

Matthew 9:11

Personal Notes

SEEING GOD

Other Thoughts

Digging Deeper

Matthew 11:18-19

Luke 7:33-35

Luke 19:1-10

John 3:16

Romans 3:23

Romans 6:23

1 Corinthians 15:3

2 Corinthians 5:21

Ephesians 2:1-10

James 5:19-20

Leadership Multiplication:
Days 26–50

A Night of Prayer

This phase in Jesus' life is focused on leadership development. As the movement continues to grow, Jesus begins to hand-select from His disciples a few to be servant leaders of the movement. After a full night of prayer, consulting with His Father, Jesus appoints twelve men who will begin their apprenticeship as leaders and will eventually become the leaders of the movement.

This is a very important stage in the movement, and I trust you are ready to learn about leadership development from the Master. Jesus has been working now for two and a half years, building a tight bond between Himself and His disciples, calling them first to *"Come and see"* (John 1:39). During this time, He explains to them that He is the Lamb of God who takes away the sins of the world and that He is the Christ. He explains who He is from Scripture and they chose to believe in Him as the Messiah. He then challenges them to *"Follow Me"* (John 1:43). During this next stage as a Christ-followers, they learn that Jesus is not only the **way** to God but that He is the **truth**. Jesus is daily revealing to them more of who He is. He is teaching them that He is fully God and fully man, the God/Man who came to earth as the Savior of the world. Jesus spends a time growing these new believers in Him. He then issues His third call to *"Come, follow me and I will make you fishers of men"* (Matt.4:19.) During this phase of the movement Jesus challenges them to join Him as disciples, leaving everything to follow Him. He then begins to share in ministry with them — teaching them how to fish for men. He does this with on-the-job training through a series of fishing expeditions in various places and with a variety of people groups.

After a couple of years of investing in them, not just the Good News — that He was the Messiah — but sharing with them His very life, He was ready for the next step. In this next phase of leadership development, Jesus' style is radical and it flies in the face of many of the popular beliefs of leadership at the time. Get ready to see leadership Jesus-style. During this phase Jesus reveals to His committed core of disciples the Father's master plan for reaching the world. Remember, it is the Father's plan. It is God who is the Architect and Master Builder (Heb. 11:10). The plan is simple to understand, revolutionary and humanly impossible. But what is impossible with man is possible with God; but when God is the one training us, we can accomplish anything (Phil. 4:13). Come explore leadership Jesus-style.

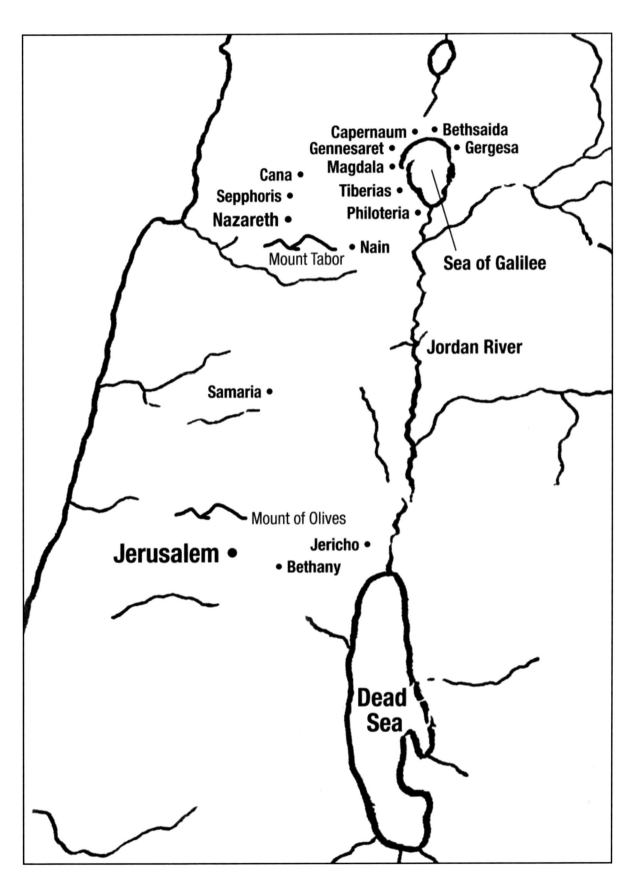

CHRONOLOGY

Choosing Apprentice Leaders

Jesus appoints twelve leaders	Luke 6:12-16; Mark 3:13-19
Jesus teaches the disciples (the Beatitudes)	Luke 6:20-49
Jesus heals the Centurion's servant	Luke 7:1-10; Matthew 8:5-13
Jesus raises widow's son	Luke 7:11-15
John doubts	Luke 7:18-23; Matthew 11:1-6
Jesus' declaration about John	Luke 7:24-35; Matthew 11:7-19
Feet washed in Simon's home	Luke 7:36-50
Jesus' second tour begins	Luke 8:1-3
Jesus calls summit with Pharisees	Matthew 12:22-45; Mark 3:20-30
Jesus tells parables	Luke 8:4-18; Matthew 13:1-53; Mark 3:20-4:35
Jesus stills the sea	Luke 8:22-25; Matthew 8:18-27; Mark 4:35-41
Jesus heals many	Luke 8:26-56; Matthew 8:28-9:34; Mark 5:1-43
Jesus sends out the twelve	Luke 9:1-6; Matthew 10:1-42; Mark 6:7-13
John beheaded and Jesus' response	Luke 9:12-17; Matthew 14:1-14; Mark 6:14-29
Jesus feeds 5,000 men	Luke 9:12-17; Matthew 14:15-23; Mark 6:35-44; John 6:4-15
Jesus walks on water	Matthew 14:22-33; Mark 6:47-52; John 6:16-21
Jesus heals in Gennesaret	Matthew 14:34-36; Mark 6:53-56
Peter's confession of Jesus	Luke 9:18-27; Matthew 16:13-20; Mark 8:27-30
Jesus feeds 4,000 men	Matthew 15:29-39; Mark 8:1-9
Jesus is transfigured	Luke 9:28-36; Matthew 17:1-13; Mark 9:2-12
Jesus attends Feast of Booths	John 7:2-53
Jesus and the adulterous woman	John 8:1-11
The validity of Jesus' testimony	John 8:12-59
Jesus heals the man born blind	John 9:1-41
Jesus the Good Shepherd	John 10:1-21
Jesus attends Feast of Tabernacles	John 10:22-39
Jesus sends out the 72	Luke 10:1-24
Jesus visits Mary and Martha	Luke 10:38-42
Jesus teaches on prayer	Luke 11:1-13
Jesus warns the people	Luke 11:14-13:9
Jesus raises Lazarus from the dead	John 11:1-43
Jesus continues to teach	Luke 13:10-17:10
Jesus en route to Jerusalem	Luke 17:11-18:34; Matthew 19:1-20; Mark 10:1-45
Jesus in Jericho	Luke 18:35-19:28; Matthew 20:29-34; Mark 10:46-52

CHRONOLOGY

Sending Proven Multipliers

Jesus anointed by Mary, Lazarus' sister	John 12:1-11
Jesus enters Jerusalem	Luke 19:12-19; Matthew 21:1-11; Mark 11:1-11; John 12:12-19
Jesus cleanses the temple (Second time)	Luke 19:45-48; Matthew 21:12-13; Mark 11:15-18
Jesus with some Greeks	John 12:20-50
Jesus and the barren fig tree	Matthew 21:18-22; Mark 11:20-25
Jesus questioned	Luke 20:1-21:4; Matthew 21:23-23:39; Mark 11:26-12:44
Signs of the end of the age	Luke 21:5-36; Matthew 24:1-25:46; Mark 13:1-37
Jesus anointed at Simon's home	Matthew 26:1-13; Mark 14:1-9
Judas agrees to betray Jesus	Luke 22:1-6; Matthew 26:14-16
Jesus' last supper with the twelve	Luke 22:7-20; Matthew 26:17-29; Mark 14:12-25; John 13:1-38
Jesus walks to the garden	John 14:1-16:33
Jesus prays	Luke 22:39-46; Matthew 26:36-46; Mark 14: 32-42; John 17:1-26
Jesus' betrayal, arrest, trial and beating	Luke 22:47-23:25; Matthew 26:47-27:26; Mark 14:43-15:20; John 18:1-19:16
Jesus' death and burial	Luke 23:26-56; Matthew 27:31-66; Mark 15:20-47; John 19:17-42
Jesus appears to His many disciples	Luke 24:1-49; Matthew 28:1-17; Mark 16:1-18; John 20:1-31; I Corinthians 15:3-8
Jesus and the last breakfast	John 21:1-15
Jesus gives the Everyday Commission	Matthew 28:16-20
Jesus' ascension into heaven in front of eleven	Luke 24:50-53; Acts 1:3-11
Jesus appears to Saul	Acts 9:1-6

DAY 26 | Choosing Leaders

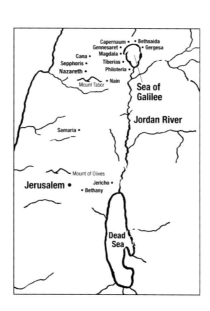

As Jesus moves into this new phase, He knows it is crucial that He listen carefully to His Father in order for the movement to expand according to the Father's master plan. Jesus called an isolated (perhaps secretive) meeting with His disciples from every area He has been in over the past two years. Probably some 120 disciples move quietly to the mountains of Naphtali just northwest of Capernaum. As they are arriving from all over, Jesus climbs to a high spot. What will He do? What will He say? What will be the next step His Father will ask Him to take? Let's take a look.

Read: Luke 6:12-19; Mark 3:13-19.

Luke 6:12 says that Jesus spent the night in prayer before choosing His leaders. What is this telling us? What do you imagine He prayed about?

What do you know about these twelve apostles?

What does the text tell us about why and how Jesus chose leaders (Mark 3:14-15)?

What do you imagine Jesus is feeling during this time?

What other questions do you still have?

Apostle and High Priest

"Therefore, holy brothers, who share in the heavenly calling, fix your thoughts on Jesus, the apostle and high priest whom we confess."

Hebrews 3:1

Personal Notes

Outside the Box

Jesus must have been excited — the ministry was growing like crazy and people from all over were believing in Him as Messiah. The movement was gaining momentum. It is at this crucial time that Jesus issues a call for His disciples to gather so that He can instruct them in the next step. The air is filled with anticipation as they gather. All must have come anticipating a strategy of liberation from the Roman oppression. After all, that was what the Messiah was all about — liberty. Why was Jesus calling them together? Would Jesus organize them in small assault teams to attack the Romans on the roads? Or would they go to Jerusalem and start the siege from there?

As they are arriving from all over Israel, Jesus climbs to the mountaintop and spends the whole night in prayer, modeling for us the first principle of leadership development — dependency on God. Jesus spends the whole night talking with His Dad, seeking His face and asking Him for the next steps. Remember this or otherwise you are headed for disaster as you develop leaders. Luke says that Jesus then came down the mountain to a level place where there was the large crowd of His disciples. How many were there? I don't know, but I am guessing some 120-150 disciples. What we do know is that Jesus descends to this level place and He publicly appoints the first twelve leaders of the movement and gives them the new name of "apostle." This gives us the second principle in choosing leaders — public appointment. Always appoint leaders in front of other disciples. Jesus shows us another key principle here: that leaders are selected from the group of disciples, not from the Christ-followers or the new believer group. Leaders are chosen from among the workers or disciples in the movement.

Notice also the twofold purpose that Jesus gives for choosing His leaders (Mark 3:14). Go ahead — look back and pick them out. Jesus chooses leaders so that, first of all, they might be with Him. He wants to draw them into a closer and more intimate relationship with Him, so that they might receive the training in servant leadership that He is ready to offer them. Secondly, He appoints them so that He might send them out to preach. Wow! The reason we call people into leadership is to draw them into a more intimate relationship with Jesus with the end goal of sending them out to preach and make more disciples. You can see that Jesus had a specific goal in mind when He called these twelve men. He wants them to go deeper into who He is and then send them out, depending on the Father, to spread the movement around the world. How will this new movement respond to these appointments? Will these men be accepted as the leaders and respected?

Live It Out

For the next several weeks we will be exploring leadership, Jesus-style. I want to challenge you that this is not just a leadership style for the church but for all of life — leadership in the home, the work place and the church. Jesus' principles of leadership may seem upside down at times, but they produce incredible results that always glorify the Father. Spend some time talking with one of your own disciples about what you have learned today on choosing leaders. Share the keys to Jesus' style of choosing leaders and discuss what character qualities Jesus was looking for in His leaders.

Other Thoughts

Digging Deeper

What did all of these twelve new leaders have in common?

Why were they chosen and not others?

Why twelve leaders?
Luke 10:1-16

Acts 14:23

2 Corinthians 8:16-24

1 Corinthians 15:3-11

What was Jesus looking for in potential leaders?
Titus 1:5-9

1 Timothy 2:5-7

1 Timothy 3:1-7

DAY 27 | Leadership Expectations

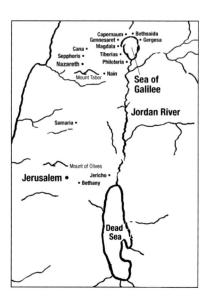

When we left Jesus yesterday He had just announced the appointment of twelve leaders. I am not sure that everyone was happy with the final decision. What about the women disciples? Yes, there were many women who were not just Christ-followers, but also disciples. In Luke 8:1-3 we have a list of several of these women. As Jesus looks into the faces of those not chosen as well as those who were chosen, I am sure He saw many different expressions. Maybe everyone expected Peter, but how about Matthew, the tax collector? Surely some people had a hard time with this selection. After all, Matthew was a traitor to his people and hated — how could Jesus choose him? And how about the fact that eleven of the twelve were from the region of Galilee? As Jesus looks out over this large crowd of disciples he shares the following:

Read: Luke 6:20-26.

As Jesus preaches this "ordination sermon," who is He looking at (Luke 6:20)? How do you visualize this?

What is Jesus modeling for us about leadership?

What was Jesus saying that leaders should expect from the ministry?

What other questions do you still have?

Outside the Box

Jesus turns His gaze toward the large crowd of disciples, who are most likely sitting on the ground, as He announces the leadership team. He then gives an incredible teaching on the expectations. Why expectations? I think one of the things that puts us in the most trouble is our own false expectations. We enter into a relationship or a new job with certain expectations, but soon we realize that the other person or boss has different expectations and we get discouraged because we did not really know what to expect. Jesus foresees this problem with leadership and addresses it right from the beginning.

A key principle in leadership is to state clearly your expectations. Let me help you unwrap the eight expectations of a leader that Jesus lays out to His team.

Expectation #1: Expect to experience poverty in the ministry, times when you will not have a dime to your name. And when these times happen, remember that you are blessed (Luke 6:20). Poverty is a gift from the Father to keep you God-dependent — don't reject it, but embrace it.

Expectation #2: Expect to experience riches in the ministry, times when God will open the flood gates and pour out so much on you that you will have a tendency to think you deserve what He is giving you. But be careful in these times of wealth, so you do not forget Who is blessing you (Luke 6:24).

Expectation #3: Expect to experience hunger in the ministry, times when you will have nothing to eat and your stomach will be growling. When that happens, remember that you are blessed (Luke 6:21). Hunger is a gift from the Father to cause you to remember that it is not by bread alone that a leader lives, but by every word that proceeds out of His mouth (Matt. 4:4).

Expectation #4: Expect to experience being full in the ministry, having times when you will eat like a king, and at times with kings and rulers. But be careful that when those times come that you do not forget the Bread of Life that satisfies your hunger forever (Luke 6:25).

Expectation #5: Expect to experience pain in the ministry, times when you will weep deeply. When that happens, remember that you are blessed (Luke 6:21). Pain is a gift from the Father to cause you to remember that we do not weep as those of this world — without hope — because we have an anchor for the soul in Jesus (Heb. 6:19).

Expectation #6: Expect to experience laughter in the ministry, times when you will laugh until your stomach hurts at the funny things that will happen as you make disciples. But be careful when those times come that you do not forget to share in the pain of others and bear each others' burdens (Luke 6:25).

Expectation #7: Expect to be hated, ostracized, insulted and scorned in the ministry for the name of Christ. There will be times when you will experience persecution for the name of Jesus and when that happens, rejoice because you are blessed (Luke 6:22-23). Persecution is a gift from the Father and a promise for all those who will live like Jesus (2 Tim. 3:12).

Expectation #8: Expect to experience being spoken well of in the ministry, when people will praise you for what God has done in and through you. But be careful when those times come that you don't receive the glory (Luke 6:26), because God shares His glory with no man (Isa. 48:11).

Immanuel

"Therefore the Lord himself will give you a sign: The virgin will be with child and will give birth to a son, and will call him Immanuel."

Isaiah 7:14

Personal Notes

SEEING GOD

Live It Out

Those who are true disciples of Jesus are promised tough times on this earth. Why? The answer is simple — hard times of poverty, hunger, tears and persecution come because they are what the Father uses to mold us and shape us into the image of His dear Son, Jesus. The Father's job in your life is to make you like Jesus (Rom. 8:29). My job and yours is to simply submit to the Father and allow Him to transform us. Share this with a friend today. Discuss your expectations in life and compare them with the expectations of a true disciple.

Other Thoughts

Digging Deeper

Matthew 5:1-20

2 Corinthians 11:23-33

Philippians 3:7-17

1 Timothy 2:5-7

2 Timothy 3:12

Titus 1:5-9

Hebrews 6:19

DAY 28 | The Father's Plan

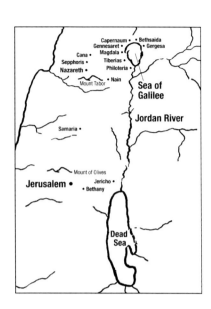

After letting His disciples know what they should expect as they leave this mountaintop experience with Him, He turns His attention to explaining the Father's plan for reaching the world. I imagine the atmosphere was electrifying with everyone shouting, "Let's take the world!" Jesus quiets them and begins sharing the game plan to bring freedom from Rome and the curse of sin. They all listen with great anticipation to the new plan. It is an awesome plan and one Jesus will explain and live out in front of His new leaders and disciples over the coming two years. It will end in the ultimate act of love — His own death. Get ready to have your world rocked!

Read: Luke 6:27-49.

As you read this passage, how would you identify the core value of this kingdom movement?

In what way was this radical love to be expressed?

Two illustrations are given in Luke 6:43-49. What are these illustrations saying to us?

Today, what are some practical ways in which you can live out radical love?

What other questions do you still have?

Rock

"They all ate the same spiritual food and drank the same spiritual drink; for they drank from the spiritual rock that accompanied them, and that rock was Christ."

1 Corinthians 10:3-4

Personal Notes

Outside the Box

Wow! Did you understand the plan? It isn't rocket science, is it? The plan is so simple and yet so revolutionary. Jesus unveils to His new leaders the team plan, which, simply put, is something like, "Don't kill a Roman; hug a Roman." From the world's standpoint, it is a crazy plan, to **love your enemies.** How in the world will loving my enemy ever bring about change, freedom and liberation? It must have sounded to them like the craziest plan in the world. It still sounds crazy 2,000 years later. How can loving my enemy free me from him? But did you read the plan carefully? It is a radical type of love. It is not human love, which always has some kind of return tied into it. It is a love that expects nothing in return (Luke 6:35). It is this radical, supernatural, God-like kind of love that will change the world. Are you ready to put it into practice? Why not give it a try? But how? How does it work? Good question — one I think those first disciples had as well.

Look again at Luke 6:37-38. In these verses, we see Jesus' idea of how to put this love into practice. He says to first stop judging other people. In order to express this love, you have to stop taking over God's job as Judge. Second, you have to stop condemning people for their actions. Instead, you need to freely extend forgiveness in Jesus' name — not because they deserve it, but because Jesus instructs us to. That is how you show your enemies love — not by judging or condemning them, but by extending forgiveness to them. Don't think this is easy. If you do, you have missed the point. Remember, for these early disciples, the Romans were one of their enemies. They had family and friends that had lost fingers for not being able to pay their taxes, knew people who had died at the hands of the Romans and seen women who had been raped. For them to not condemn, but extend forgiveness was no human act. It is a kind of love that can only be brought about by God.

Their faces must have shown how shocked they were as Jesus revealed the Father's plan for the defeat of Rome. I can only imagine how deflated they must have felt as Jesus revealed this plan to His excited, anxious and hurting disciples. Then He turned to His leaders and told them that the blind cannot lead the blind (Luke 6:39), so He expects them to take the lead in this supernatural forgiveness. The next thing he says is so amazing: *"A student is not above his teacher, but everyone who is fully trained will be like his teacher."* Wow. Mark it down. It starts with Jesus — he is the teacher that will show them the way. He will live this lifestyle of supernatural forgiveness and train them to do the same. Let it be noted that, in my humble opinion, it is this supernatural love that brought down the Roman empire even as the early church demonstrated that love by voluntarily giving their lives for the cause of Christ and forgiving their killers.

Jesus then tells them to stop judging others' sins and start doing some self-examining of their own hearts. For it is out of the heart that the mouth speaks forgiveness. At this point I can only imagine the expressions on the faces of these disciples. Jesus ends this Leadership 101 class by saying to those first disciples, "Why call me your Lord if you are not even going to listen to what I teach you?" Go out now to return to your homes and obey Me. Love your enemies! Do this by offering them undeserved forgiveness, instead of judgment and condemnation, and the movement will multiply rapidly."

Live It Out

Do you want to see God's hand in your life? Then obey Him. Who is your enemy? Make a list. It can be people close and far away. It doesn't matter how long the list is, just be honest. Between you and God, who is someone you have been condemning in your own mind? That is your enemy. We do this almost every single day. We hold court in our own minds on others' motives, attitudes and actions, without ever even knowing all the facts. We judge them guilty, and then we pass judgment and hand out our own sentence of silence, gossip or worse.

Now the tough part! Give it a try. Pick one person on your list and extend forgiveness to them today. Then get with a disciple and talk about this outrageous plan of love. Ask God to search your heart and reveal your judgmental attitudes, confess them and receive His forgiveness.

Other Thoughts

Digging Deeper

Deuteronomy 6:4-9

Matthew 5:43-48

Matthew 10:37-39

Matthew 22:37-40

John 13:34-35

John 15:10-17

1 Corinthians 13:1-13

1 John 3:1-3

DAY 29 | Leadership and Authority

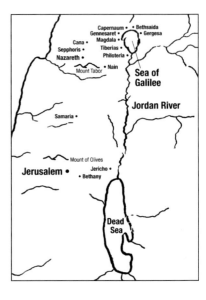

After choosing the first leaders for the movement and laying out the Father's plan for reaching the world, Jesus comes down from the mountain and returns to His home and ministry center in Capernaum. His leaders are now with Him almost 24/7. And who does the Father have waiting in the wings but a Roman centurion? Oh, the humor of our Father in Heaven! How will Jesus model His new leadership style? How will it all play out?

Read: Luke 7:1-10; Matthew 8:5-13.

What do we know about centurions?

What character qualities do we see in this centurion?

What is this Gentile soldier modeling for us about leadership?

What was Jesus' response to this centurion? Why?

What other questions do you still have?

Outside the Box

As we begin today, I just want to remind you that we are sticking with Luke as the primary source in our chronological study, mainly because Luke tells us that it was his intent to put the events of Jesus' life in a chronological form. You will note that Matthew, on the other hand, gives us three chapters (Matthew 5-7) of all the things Jesus had been teaching for the first two years of ministry, and then begins to tell how Jesus modeled what He taught in the following chapters. Don't get confused; Matthew just had a different way of organizing the information. But both authors are giving an accurate account, only from different points of view.

Have you ever wondered if God gets caught off guard? I wonder if Jesus here was not caught by surprise at the Father's sense of humor. It says in Luke 7:9 that Jesus marveled at this centurion. I find it ironic and a bit funny that it is a Roman centurion, the enemy and a leader in one of the most brutal armies this world has ever known, that is about to be used by God to teach our next four leadership principles. He was a Roman leader, sent by Rome to maintain order, enforce the laws and collect the taxes. He will be God's instrument of instruction for these new leaders. Notice the love this leader must have had for His slave (Luke 7:2), to send friends to find Jesus and ask for His help. Notice also that it says that this centurion loved the people of Israel and had built the synagogue in Capernaum (Luke 7:5). **Principle #1:** A leader loves those they are leading, hurts for them and cares for them.

Next, notice the humility of this Gentile. He sends the Jewish elders and then some friends to implore Jesus to help. But notice what he tells them to say: *"'Lord, don't trouble yourself, for I do not deserve to have you come under my roof. That is why I did not even consider myself worthy to come to you'"* (Luke 7:6-7). **Principle #2:** A leader leads with humility, realizing that they are not worthy of the great honor of serving as a leader in the army of the Lord God of Hosts.

Thirdly, notice the faith of this foreigner. He says, *"'But say the word, and my servant will be healed'"* (Luke 7:7). It shocks Jesus and He declares, *"'I tell you, I have not found such great faith even in Israel'"* (Luke 7:9). **Principle #3:** A leader leads by faith, trusting not in what their physical eyes see, but in the Invisible God, with whom all things are possible.

Lastly, note the understanding of the lines of authority by this solider. He says, *"'For I myself am a man under authority, with soldiers under me'"* (Luke 7:8). This man knew that he was a leader and he knew how to lead, but he never forgot that he himself was also under authority and would need to give an account to his superiors of how he led. **Principle #4:** A leader never forgets that they are also under authority and will give an account for how they led the people God has placed under their care. You have authority only as you are under authority.

Live It Out

Love, humility, faith and authority are all principles of godly leadership, modeled by Jesus and a centurion some 2,000 years ago. What kind of leader will you be? Talk with your disciple today about leadership and these four principles. Commit to be a leader like Jesus.

Author and Perfecter of Faith

"Let us fix our eyes on Jesus, the author and perfecter of our faith, who for the joy set before him endured the cross, scorning its shame, and sat down at the right hand of the throne of God."

Hebrews 12:2

Personal Notes

SEEING GOD

Other Thoughts

Digging Deeper

Love:

John 13:1-20

1 Corinthians 13:1-13

Humility:

Matthew 11:29

Philippians 2:5-11

1 Peter 5:1-6

Faith:

Hebrews 11:1-40

Galatians 2:20

1 Timothy 4:12

Authority:

Romans 13:1-7

Hebrews 13:17

1 Peter 2:13-17

DAY 30 | Leadership Misunderstood

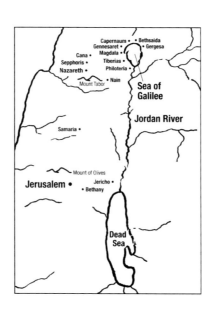

Wow! I hope you are wrestling with leading like Jesus. I so want to be a leader that loves, is humble, has great faith in God and who knows who his authority is. I struggle with all four aspects of leadership and so need Jesus living in me and through me to be the leader He calls me to be. Note also that as we work our way through this study in the life of Christ, I was forced to pick only fifty events, thus we will be leaving out important events like the one found in Luke 7:11-17 when Jesus shows the power and authority over the dead by raising a widow's son to life.

Jesus was often misunderstood as a leader. In today's study, Jesus pays tribute to another greatly unappreciated and misunderstood leader. He honors this leader who was both His dear friend and co-laborer in the Kingdom of God. Come learn some more from the Master about leadership.

Read: Luke 7:18-35; Matthew 11:2-19.

What do we know at this point about John the Baptist?

Why did John send his disciples to Jesus?

Why was John doubting?

How is John the Baptist honored by Jesus?

Friend of Sinners

"The Son of Man came eating and drinking, and they say, 'Here is a glutton and a drunkard, a friend of tax collectors and "sinners." But wisdom is proved right by her actions.'"

Matthew 11:19

Personal Notes

What is Jesus modeling for us about leadership?

What other questions do you still have?

Outside the Box

John the Baptist is sitting in prison, and he is having some doubts as to whether or not Jesus is the Expected One. How can this be, a leader doubting? Yes, John, who is sitting on a cold prison floor in Herod's cell, is having serious doubts about the facts that he was previously proclaiming: that Jesus is the One (John 1:26,27,29). John, who had been telling people for over three years that Jesus is the Messiah and the Lamb of God, is doubting. So he sends some of his loyal disciples to ask Jesus a very heart-wrenching question, *"'Are you the one who was to come, or should we expect someone else?'"* (Luke 7:19). Leaders sometimes doubt even the very things they have clung to for a long time. Why was John doubting?

I do not have space to go into a long discussion, only to point out a few facts to you. In Luke, we read that John's disciples were reporting to John all that Jesus was saying and doing.

In Matthew, we read that when John heard what Jesus was saying, He began to question. Thus, there must have been something Jesus was saying that caused John to doubt the Master. In the Digging Deeper section, you will find passages that will help you discover why John is doubting. I challenge you to dig deeper. Notice that when John's disciples arrive Jesus is in the middle of teaching the crowd; they interrupt Him to tell Him what John sent them for. Everyone present hears that about John's doubts. Can you imagine the looks on the faces of the newly chosen leaders and Jesus' disciples? Remember that many of these disciples were former disciples of John (John 1:35-37). In fact, it was John who had pointed them to Jesus. How could it be that John is now going through this?

Jesus responds to John's doubts with a passage from Scripture with a hidden meaning. It was obvious code between Jesus and John, and somehow Jesus knew that when John heard these words he would say, *"Yes — Jesus is the Messiah!"* Jesus sends the messengers not with a yes or no answer but with an Old Testament scripture from Isaiah 61:1-2 and 35:5, the same section Jesus read back in Nazareth when he was rejected by His own town's people.

Jesus then turns to the silent crowd and pays John an incredible tribute. Jesus says, *"'Among those born of women there has not risen anyone greater than John the Baptist ...'"* (Matt. 11:11). If nothing else, this statement by Jesus should make you want to go back and find out who this guy was. If you do, you will find a leader with deep love, humility, faith and a clear understanding of authority, just the type of leader the Father is looking for. Yet, they said of John, *"'He has a demon'"* (Matt. 11:18). John was so misunderstood in his day and even today. Most people still have the image of John as a wild man running around in the wilderness dressed unfashionably and eating locusts and wild honey.

Jesus, too, was greatly misunderstood in His day and even today. Hopefully you are learning that not only is Jesus your Savior and the way to a personal relationship with the Father, but He is much more. He is the truth and He is the Life. Did you catch the phrase that they pinned on Jesus after watching Him for two years in ministry? It is in Matthew 11:19. Look back at it and let it sink in. After two years of watching Jesus' life from afar, the religious leaders and the people made a very astute observation. They said of Jesus, *"'Here is a glutton and a drunkard, a friend of tax collectors and "sinners."'"* They got part of it right at least. While Jesus was not a glutton nor a drunkard, He most certainly was a friend of tax collectors and sinners. Thank God that Jesus loved sinners or where would I be? Where would you be? Know that as a leader, you will often be misunderstood. It is part of leadership. Often your actions and words will be misconstrued or taken out of context and used against you, like they are being done here against Jesus. Relax, it happened to the best. You are in good company.

Live It Out

How about you? What are you known as? Do sinners call you their friend? Do you spend enough time reaching out to non-believers that sometimes others misunderstand you and call you a friend of sinners? It is something to think about! Spend some time today discussing with one of your disciples what you learned today.

Take a few moments and thank God for the leaders in your life, those who have invested so much in you. Take a few minutes and write them a note telling them how much you appreciate their investment in you.

Other Thoughts

SEEING GOD

Digging Deeper

Isaiah 40:3

Malachi 4:5-6

Luke 1:1-25

Luke 1:57-80

Luke 3:1-20

Mark 1:1-8

Matthew 14:1-12

Matthew 17:10-13

Life of Elijah — 1 Kings 17- 2 Kings 2/Matthew 11:14

DAY 31 | Forgiveness and Leadership

It appears that there is a curious Pharisee living in Capernaum, who has been following the ministry of Jesus. He is intrigued enough to risk his reputation and invite Jesus over for a meal with some of his friends. Jesus accepts the invitation and what transpires is nothing less than life transforming. Take a look!

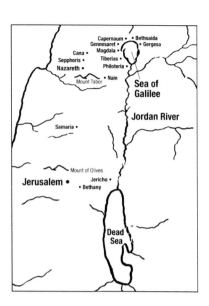

Read: Luke 7:36-50.

What does this passage tell us about Simon the Pharisee (a religious leader of the day)?

What does this "sinful woman" do that demonstrated real leadership humility?

What were the disciples learning about leadership Jesus-style?

What is this passage telling us about how we should love?

What other questions do you still have?

King of Kings

"...which God will bring about in his own time — God, the blessed and only Ruler, the King of kings and Lord of lords..."

1 Timothy 6:15

Personal Notes

Outside the Box

Maybe Simon the Pharisee was one of the elders who came to Jesus in Luke 7 to ask Him to heal the centurion's slave. Or maybe he had been in Jerusalem and seen Jesus' burst of outrage. We can almost certainly be sure that he was one of the Pharisees in Chapter 5 because of the topic of discussion that he and Jesus have. Remember the theme of the discussion a few months earlier?

The Pharisees had come wanting to know if Jesus would say that He had the power to forgive sins. Jesus responds, *"'But that you may know that the Son of Man has authority on earth to forgive sins ... I tell you, get up ...'"* (Luke 5:24). This miracle and Jesus' response must have been lingering in the mind of this man and he wanted to know more. I also wonder who gave this story to Luke? I mean, who was the eyewitness that told Luke about what happened this day in Simon's house? Maybe, just maybe, it was one of these two sinners that Jesus is going to reach out to.

Anyway, Jesus accepts Simon's kind invitation and the Father's divine appointment to reach out to this religious, self-righteous man and teach us something about leadership all at the same time. There were three customary things that this woman does for Jesus that Simon did not. Did you pick up on them? They are in Luke 7:44-46 — a foot washing, a kiss and an anointing. All three of these were Jewish customs for someone who was a guest of honor. Simon did not do this, so the Father sent a sinful woman to do it for His beloved Son. What a gift! Notice how, throughout Jesus' life, His Father continued to send all kinds of gifts His way. Today, we see a beautiful gift wrapped in a dirty, sinful package. Jesus receives the gift from His Father as this woman humbles herself and lavishes Jesus with an expensive bath of tears and alabaster oil, much to Simon the Pharisees' displeasure.

Thus, Jesus gives Simon a short story with a deep and abiding principle. The story is of two people who have a debt they cannot pay, just like you and me. I had a debt I could not pay; He paid a debt He did not owe. Jesus then asks Simon a question and he gives a great answer. The person who has been forgiven more (or at least thinks they have) loves more. You see, the woman knew she was a big sinner. She was honest and came seeking forgiveness from Jesus. Simon, on the other hand, really didn't consider himself much of a sinner, at least not to the degree of this woman. After all, he kept the law and gave an outward impression of having a good, sin-free life. Yet the truth was that Simon was just as big a sinner as this woman, except he didn't realize it. He was self-deceived. He had learned through his religious system how to cover his sins up, to keep them behind closed doors so that no one would know what a hypocrite he was. As a leader, don't fall into the trap of hiding your sins — confess them one to another and pray for one another (James 5:16). Consider what Jesus is saying. If you do not feel you have been forgiven much, your love for Jesus will never be very intense. You have to come to grips with your own sinfulness, even if you have not physically killed, raped someone or committed adultery. Take a hard look at your thought life if you are struggling to see yourself as God does. You are a vile creature and all your good works are as filthy rags in God's sight. Get over yourself. Start dying to the old self and living to God.

Live It Out

When was the last time you anointed Jesus with a gift like that of the woman in today's story? When did you last give Jesus a foot washing, a kiss or an anointing with oil? Jesus said, *"'For I was hungry and you gave me something to eat, I was thirsty and you gave me something to drink…Then the righteous will answer him, 'Lord, when did we see you hungry and feed you, or thirsty and give you something to drink?'…The King will reply, 'I tell you the truth, whatever you did for one of the least of these brothers of mine, you did for me'"* (Matt. 25:35-40). How do you wash Jesus' feet, kiss Him, or anoint Him with oil? Do it to one another. Go to one of your disciples today and wash their feet, give them a hug or anoint them with oil and do it in Jesus' name and you have done it to Jesus Himself. Go for it!

Other Thoughts

Digging Deeper

Nehemiah 9:17

Psalms 130:4

Isaiah 55:7

Jonah 4:2

Matthew 18:21-35

Luke 11:1-4

Luke 17:1-4

Ephesians 1:7

Colossians 1:13,14

Hebrews 9:22-28

SEEING GOD

DAY 32 | Leadership and Faith

Have you ever been so tired that you slept right through a storm? That is where we find Jesus today. As the movement continues to expand, Jesus finds it harder and harder to find a place to rest or even get a bite to eat. In Mark 3:20, Peter notes *"Then Jesus entered a house, and again a crowd gathered, so that he and his disciples were not even able to eat."* Luke records, probably from Mary's memories, *"Now Jesus' mother and brothers came to see him, but they were not able to get near him because of the crowd"* (Luke 8:19). Can you imagine how hard it must have been to constantly come back to a full house and growing crowds? Where could Jesus escape or get away from the crowds? Come and see!

Read: Luke 8:22-25; Matthew 8:18-27; Mark 4:35-41.

List what you feel are the major details of this story (look at all three passages carefully).

What did the *"other side"* mean to the disciples (Mark 4:35)? Who was there?

What was the real problem in this story? List all the small and large problems in the disciples' minds.

Why do you feel God allowed this storm? What are the life lessons from this story that the disciples needed to learn?

What other questions do you still have?

Outside the Box

Wow! Jesus must have been one incredibly tired guy to be able to sleep through a storm where professional fishermen thought they were about to lose their lives just sailing in it! Can you see the humanity of Jesus through it all? Yes, Jesus got tired just like we do. He got hungry and thirsty, just like us. He experienced things physically, emotionally and spiritually. Jesus was fully human. Wow! God fully became one of His own creations, like us in every way and yet without sin (Heb. 2:17). The God/Man needed a break, a rest from the ministry. Mark it down — the bigger the ministry gets, the more intentional you will need to be in getting time away to rest. Ministry can be all-consuming and extremely demanding. You will get tired and need to escape as Jesus does to get refreshed.

As the movement grows, we will see Jesus using the Sea of Galilee as a place to escape and recuperate with His leaders. Much of the next year of ministry will happen on and around the shore of this body of water. Jesus often gets in the boat, not to get to the other side of the lake, but to simply escape the pressure of the crowds. This didn't happen because He did not love the people, but because He wanted to be alone with His leaders to make a point. Both are the case today as you read about the storm. Mark records that Jesus left the crowds and that there were a number of boats in this excursion. Jesus goes immediately to the stern of the boat and falls asleep on a cushion. He was sound asleep in minutes. As they move across the lake, the Father sent a strong wind that started to make the water pour into the boat. The leaders were scared for their lives. Can you imagine the conversation between the leaders? "You wake Him!" "Not me — why don't you wake Him?" "I'm not going to wake Him up now."

Finally, it is too much and they are sure they are going to drown. They scream, *"Lord, save us!"* (Matt. 8:25). These are words Jesus loves to hear. All you have to do is cry out, "I can't do this! Save me!" And He is right there for you. One of my favorite verses is Zephaniah 3:17, which says *"The LORD your God is with you, he is mighty to save. He will take great delight in you, he will quiet you with his love, he will rejoice over you with singing."* Wow!

After saving the day, Jesus looks at them and says, "Guys, where is your faith?" (Luke 8:25). He questions their faith. He didn't expect them to still the storm. He just expected them to know Him well enough by now to know that He is never too busy or too tired to save the day. No matter how much you call on Him, He never grows weary of helping you. That is why He came to earth!

Live It Out

Got any storms in your life? Maybe you have a stormy relationship or a storm at work? Stop fighting the storm and worrying about it; instead, fall on your knees and admit you need Mighty Warrior to save you. He waits every day for you to come to the end of yourself and start depending on Him. Spend some time today talking to one of your disciples about living by faith in dependence on and obedience to the Father. Practice saying **"God, save the day!"** in the midst of the storms in your life.

A Mighty Warrior

"The Lord your God is with you, he is mighty to save. He will take great delight in you, he will quiet you with his love, he will rejoice over you with singing."

Zephaniah 3:17

Personal Notes

SEEING GOD

Other Thoughts

Digging Deeper

Hebrews 11:6

Romans 14:23

1 Thessalonians 5:24

2 Timothy 2:2-13

James 1:5-6

James 2:14-26

Revelation 19:11

DAY 33 | Sending Leaders

After months of intensive leadership training, it is finally time for the twelve apprentices to be sent out on their own mission trip. Remember, Jesus called these twelve guys for two reasons: first, so that they might be with Him and grow closer to him and second, so that He might send them out (Mark 3:14). It is no surprise to them that Jesus is sending them out. It is an exciting time, and yet the twelve are scared to death. How will they respond to the challenge? Where will Jesus send them? What will He say to them and what will happen? Check it out!

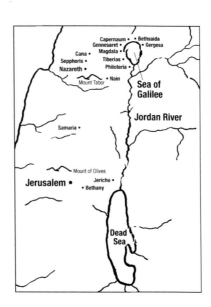

Read: Luke 9:1-6; Matthew 10:5-23; Mark 6:7-13.

Preparatory to this story is Matthew 9:35-38. What was happening in the heart of Jesus in those verses?

As the twelve listened to Jesus instruct them, what do you think they were feeling? What questions did they probably have?

What are Jesus' instructions before he sends them out?

What lessons do you think they learned from this mission trip?

What other questions do you still have?

The Way

"Jesus answered, I am the way and the truth and the life. No one comes to the Father except through me."

John 14:6

Personal Notes

Outside the Box

I think that Jesus waited until the night before to tell His disciples, "In the morning, I will send you out on a trip. Come ready for the adventure of a lifetime! Get a good night's rest, because you will need it." I imagine they did not sleep much that night as their minds raced with questions about the coming adventure. As day breaks, they assemble around the fire and get a little breakfast. Jesus mingles among them and embraces each one. He notes what each one has brought for their journey. He quiets the twelve down and has them take a seat on the ground. A few last words of instruction and they will be ready to go. This was the culmination of His promise to them that He would send them out (Mark 3:14). I am sure some thought they were ready and others were scared and very unsure of what was about to happen. What did he tell them before sending them off?

"First," Jesus said, "drop everything you packed for the journey on the ground in front of you. You won't need it! Take nothing! You won't need that staff, Peter, and you can leave that bag, John. James, that loaf of bread in your pocket can stay behind. And Matthew, you will not need any of your money. No extra tunics, Andrew. Just leave everything here. I will be praying for you. You will go out like sheep among the wolves, but you will see great things!"

Why would Jesus send them out without the minimal creature comforts? What could He possibly be wanting to teach these leaders?

I believe He wanted to teach them dependency on the Father. He sent them out just like the Father had sent Him into the world, in complete dependence on God for everything that they would need. This was a crucial time in the movement. Would they depend on the Father? Not just for their physical needs, but even for the words that would come out of their mouths? He instructed them: *"'... do not worry about what to say or how to say it. At that time you will be given what to say, for it will not be you speaking, but the Spirit of your Father speaking through you"* (Matt. 10:19-20). Wow! This experience is to teach them to fully depend on the Father. Jesus so wanted them to understand that if they would only have faith in the Father, He would provide everything they needed. Remember the expectations He gave them months before in Luke 6:20-22? He said you are blessed when you are poor, hungry, weeping and people are speaking evil of you. Each of the things they leave behind corresponds to something from Luke 6.

Jesus then gives them instructions about how they are to enter the cities and villages and where exactly they are supposed to go. This is a mission trip to the lost sheep of Israel (Matt. 10:5-6). This mission trip is to be within their own country, to people who look like them and speak their own language. It is their first step — to take the gospel to their own people. The transcultural trips are coming, but for now the focus is on Israeli settlements and Jewish people. Jesus gives many more instructions on what house to enter, what exactly to say, how long to stay and when to move on. He even instructs them as to how to respond when persecuted for the message. It is like a training manual about how to do short-term missions within your own culture. This experience is meant to teach these young leaders complete dependence on the Father.

Finally, Jesus pairs them up and sends them out. I wonder how Jesus paired them up? Who went with whom? Did Peter draw Matthew? That would have been some trip. I can only imagine the emotions that filled that place as pair by pair set off in different directions. Six pairs of two on the adventure of a lifetime, taking the Good News of the Kingdom to lost Jewish people. I imagine that Jesus called each pair forward and gave them specific instructions as to where to go, when to return and then prayed over each one. Jesus left without the twelve guys He had invested in as leaders for the last months. What will Jesus do as they are away for the next several weeks?

Live It Out

Have you ever been on a short-term mission trip within your own country? If not, I would highly encourage it. I know it has changed my life and the lives of my own disciples. Now you have the instruction manual for this kind of experience. Why not plan one with some of your disciples? It doesn't have to be some huge, expensive thing. It is simple — just go out with the gospel and nothing else. You will be trusting God to provide for everything you will need. You do not need to raise money before or during the trip. Remember, it is a trip in your own area, with people who speak your language and have your same customs. I can guarantee one thing if you take on this challenge: it will be an adventure. I imagine for most of you this will scare the life out of you as it did for most of the disciples. Pray about it and chat with your disciples as you look at this passage together. Then take a risk and set a date.

Other Thoughts

Digging Deeper

Read Luke 6:20-26 in connection with Luke 9:3-5.

Acts 4:1-22

Acts 13:1-4

2 Corinthians 8:1-5

Philippians 4:10-14

DAY 34 | Leading While Grieving

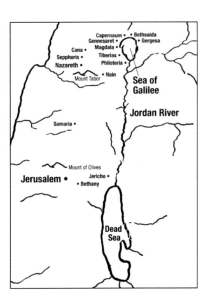

Meanwhile, as the disciples are wandering the countryside having the adventure of a lifetime, something else very exciting was happening in Israel. It was the birthday of King Herod and he was throwing a party for himself that would last for days, if not weeks. At this party something would happen that would launch the movement to a new level at a deep personal cost to Jesus Himself. Read this sad story very carefully.

Read: Matthew 14:1-14; Mark 6:14-34; Luke 9:7-11.

What do these passages tell us about Herod?

What is Herod thinking and feeling? What does he end up doing?

How does Jesus respond to the death of His best friend (Matt. 14:13)?

What emotions must Jesus be experiencing?

What other questions do you still have?

Outside the Box

When we last saw John the Baptist, he was sitting on a cold prison floor awaiting his fate and receiving the hidden message from Jesus in response to his doubts. In this account, we discover why John is in prison (Mark 6:17-18). John had publicly spoken out against King Herod for taking and marrying his brother Philip's wife while Philip was still alive. For this, he had been thrown in prison but not killed. Herod seemingly knew that John was sent from God and was a true prophet. Because of this, he was deathly afraid of John. Mark also notes that Herod liked listening to John (Mark 6:20).

King Herod threw a banquet and invited all the military commanders and upper-class people of Galilee to his palace. They all arrived and were enjoying the party when his brother's daughter danced before him. He opened his big mouth in front of all these important people and made a really stupid promise. He tells this girl that she can have whatever she wants. Not knowing what to choose, she runs over to her mom and asks the wicked woman what she should ask for. Her mother seizes the opportunity to take her vengeance on John and tells her to return and ask for the head of John on a platter. Can you imagine what type of woman would do such a thing? This is one angry woman to request that her daughter ask for the head of a man. Herod, stuck between a rock and a hard place, gives in because of his pride, so he sends for John to be beheaded in the prison and the head to be returned before the party ends. John is now dead. His disciples gathered, took his headless body and laid it in a tomb. Thet ran to Jesus to report what had happened.

As they make their way to Jesus, word is also making its way to Herod that something very strange is happening all over Israel. People are being healed, the gospel is being preached and people are being freed from demonic oppression. Herod is stunned and thinks that John has risen from the dead — his worst nightmare. In reality, it was God at work through the twelve apostles.

We learn from Matthew that as the twelve head out for their mission adventure, Jesus also departed from the place where he had sent them out and was preaching from city to city (Matt. 11:1). What was Jesus doing? I think He was busy training the next set of leaders who were waiting in the wings. They are the seventy who will be sent out in a short period of time as Jesus works to expand the movement.

The disciples return from their mission trip, full of stories of the Father's provision for them each step of the way (Luke 9:10). I imagine there were stories of success, funny things that happened, supernatural God-sightings and the persecution they encountered along the way. They may have been driven out of some cities and even stoned as they brought the message of salvation to their own people of Israel. As they share God-sightings all night long, John's disciples arrive with the news of John's incredibly brutal death (Matt. 14:12). Upon hearing the news, Jesus is grief-stricken and gets into a boat all by himself to withdraw from the crowds to be alone (Matt. 14:13). His disciples watch and wonder what Jesus will do, since they remember that this is the guy they had recently seen still the storm (Luke 8:22-25), raise people from the dead (Luke 7:11-17) and display incredible powers. He is the same man who had been teaching about forgiveness, teaching them to love their enemies by forgiving them. What will He do? The answer comes in tomorrow's reading!

Man of Sorrows

"He was despised and rejected by men, a man of sorrows, and familiar with suffering. Like one from whom men hide their faces he was despised, and we esteemed him not."

Isaiah 53:3

Personal Notes

SEEING GOD

Live It Out

Love, humility, faith and authority — these are qualities of godly leadership modeled by Jesus and a centurion some 2,000 years ago. What kind of leader will you be? Talk with your disciple today about leadership and these four qualities. Commit to be a Jesus-style leader.

Other Thoughts

Digging Deeper

Isaiah 53:1-5

Jeremiah 9:1-24

Hosea 2:1-14

Luke 22:39-46

John 11:1-45

Romans 12:15

DAY 35 | Servant Leadership

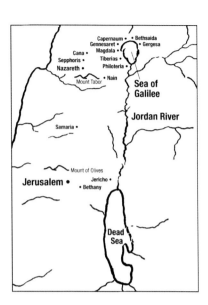

The news of John's death and the way in which he died stung like a sharp knife, piercing Jesus' soul. Grieving, Jesus retreats to the comfort of the Father and the silence of the Sea of Galilee. He tells His disciples to come with Him and He escapes to a secluded place. People were coming from everywhere after hearing the news about John's death (Mark 6:31). Some feel that this crowd is angry and ready for a revolution and a new king (John 6:15)! What is going to happen?

Read: Luke 9:12-17; Matthew 14:15-21; Mark 6:35-44; John 6:1-14. Jot down what you discover about:

Why were the crowds following Jesus?

What did the twelve want to do with these crowds?

What lessons do you think God the Father wanted the disciples to learn during this experience?

What/who made this miracle possible?

What other questions do you still have?

Good Shepherd

"'I am the good shepherd. The good shepherd lays down his life for the sheep.'"

John 10:11

Personal Notes

Outside the Box

It is abundantly clear that Jesus had every intention of crossing the Sea of Galilee to Bethsaida and retreating with His disciples to a quiet place to grieve (Luke 9:10). But the Father had a different plan, a lesson in leadership through times of personal loss and deep personal pain. From the boat, Jesus sees that the crowd is already beginning to gather and decides to dock close by. The crowd is forming for a variety of reasons. Some want to avenge John's death and make Jesus the new king (John 6:15). Others were drawn to the many miracles the disciples and Jesus were doing (John 6:2). As the crowd begins to form, Jesus takes His disciples quickly and escapes to a mountain ledge nearby, overlooking Bethsaida and the Sea of Galilee. I imagine Jesus, angry and frustrated over the seemingly senseless death of His best friend, laying prostrate on the ground, begging the Father to do something, anything. It is in this position that the Father must have said, "Son, lift up your eyes!" We do read in John 6:5 that Jesus looked and saw the incredible number of people marching toward Him. Mark 6:34 says that Jesus sees this massive crowd assembling below Him and He is moved with compassion for them, because they looked to Him like sheep without a shepherd.

As Jesus and His leaders descend the mountain to the crowd of people below, Jesus turns to Philip and asks him *"'Where shall we buy bread for these people to eat?'"* Surely Philip will respond in faith, believing God will provide a miracle. Andrew, however, who had just returned from his mission trip having seen God provide supernaturally, does some quick math, checks with Judas to see how much is in the money bag he was carrying and tells Jesus that it would take way too much money to feed the crowd. As the day wears on, Jesus teaches and ministers to the huge crowd — 5,000 men, plus women and children. Some calculate as many as 20,000 people. Wow! Now it is late and everyone is starting to get hungry. Jesus tells the twelve leaders to give the people something to eat. They ask if they should spend the 200 denarii that they obviously had to buy the bread. At this point Jesus says, *"Go, collect what you can from the people and bring it here."*

In this case, the only person who had something to give was a young man whom Andrew found. This guy was willing to give all he had — 5 barley biscuits and 2 small, sardine-size fish. With this meager offering, Jesus then has His largest outreach event, and some would argue His biggest miracle, feeding 5,000 men, plus the women and children, and having twelve baskets left over after everyone had eaten their fill. Let me unwrap the lessons of multiplication that I think Jesus is teaching His leaders: 1) **Lift up your eyes and see the need.** Multiplication begins as you get your eyes off of yourself and see the needs of others. 2) **Allow your soul to be moved to compassion** for the needs of others. 3) **Assemble the resources** you have around you. They didn't start with much, but God made it work. Was the young man the only one who had something to offer? No way! Others had food, but the difference was that they were not willing to share it. They were saving it for themselves and their families. One young man gave all he had, and God multiplied it. Someone has to give it all if you are to see multiplication happen in your world. 4) **Get organized and allow the supernatural to happen.** In our story Jesus tells the disciples to seat the people in groups of 50 or 100, making it easy for Matthew, the numbers guy, to do a quick count and give us the facts (Matt. 14:21). 5)**Offer all you have to God in faith** with thanksgiving, believing that all things are possible with God. In our story, Jesus takes the food and looks up toward heaven with eyes wide open and thanks the Father for His provision (John 6:11). 6) **Take a step of obedience** and trust God to do the supernatural.

Live It Out

Jesus divided the five biscuits and the two fish among the twelve, giving each leader some. I can only imagine the faces of these leaders as Jesus tells them to turn and distribute the food among the people. The looks had to have been priceless. But note carefully when multiplication begins. It began when the disciples obeyed and not before. As they distributed the food in faith, believing God, the miracle started happening. Think about it.

Multiplication will happen in your life the same way as it did for Jesus and His early leaders. Lift up your eyes, see the need, be filled with compassion, assemble the resources, organize your life for the miracle, offer up the resources you have in faith with thanksgiving and then, most importantly, take a step of obedience. Spend some time today discussing Jesus' principles of multiplication with the people you are investing in.

Other Thoughts

Digging Deeper

Genesis 1:22,28

1 Kings 17:8-16

2 Kings 4:1-7

Matthew 15:32-38

Matthew 25:14-30

Mark 8:1-10

Luke 19:11-27

1 Thessalonians 2:8

2 Timothy 2:2

SEEING GOD

DAY 36 | Walking on Water

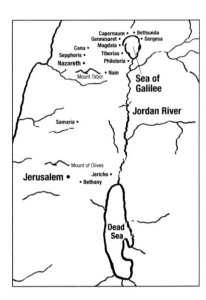

After a full day of ministry and picking up twelve baskets of leftovers, Jesus sees that the disciples are exhausted. So He sends them off in a boat, onto the Sea of Galilee to get them away from the crowd and allow them to rest, while he dismisses everyone else (Mark 6:45). After bidding the crowd farewell, Jesus makes His way back up a nearby mountain to spend some time debriefing with His Father (Mark 6:46). It has been a long day, filled with a whirlwind of emotions for Jesus. He begins to relax and is just enjoying the communion with His Father, when...

Read: Matthew 14:22-33; Mark 6:45-52; John 6:16-21.

As you study this story, what amazes you?

What might Jesus have been thinking about as He watched His disciples *"straining at the oars"*? (Mark 6:48)

What do you think Peter was thinking during this experience?

What lessons did Jesus want His disciples to learn here?

What other questions do you still have?

Outside the Box

Jesus enjoyed an incredible night of communion with His Dad. As always, He was energized after spending time in prayer. Possibly the words of Isaiah 40:31 brought Him strength, *"... but those who hope in the Lord will renew their strength. They will soar on wings like eagles; they will run and not grow weary, they will walk and not be faint."* Jesus must have realized that the people below had wanted to make Him king that morning (John 6:15). What was He to do? What were the marching orders? Jesus spent the evening discussing His next steps with His Dad.

It is late now, about three o'clock in the morning (Matthew 14:25). As the wind begins to blow, Jesus lifts up His eyes and sees His leaders out on the lake struggling against the storm. What will they do without Him? Will they exercise their faith? Jesus begins to make His way out to the disciples who are about 3-4 miles out from shore (John 6:19). As He comes close to the boat, they start screaming, "It's a ghost!" They were overtired and too scared to think about the impossibility of it actually being a ghost. When we are tired and scared, who knows what will come out of our mouths? Jesus continued to come closer and says, *"Take courage! It is I. Don't be afraid"* (Matt. 14:27).

Peter seizes the opportunity for a little adventure and says, *"Lord, if it's you, tell me to come to you on the water"* (Matt. 14:28). Jesus tells him to come. I wonder what those first few steps felt like for Peter? It must have been the coolest thing ever to step out of that boat and walk on the water. Everything is going well until Peter takes his eyes off Jesus and places them on what is happening around him. At that moment, he begins to sink. It will happen every time if we do the same. You need to keep your eyes on Jesus and not on the circumstances that surround you if you want to walk on water. I love what happens next. Jesus looks at Peter sinking and says, "Stay there a while, learn to keep your eyes on me. In fact, go under a few times and then I will think about saving you." No, he does not say that at all! Notice what Peter cries: ***"Lord, save me!"*** (Matt. 14:30). Sound familiar? I am convinced that God loves to hear those words from us; He is a Savior who loves to save the day, because when He saves the day, He gets all the glory.

So Jesus immediately stretches out His hand and lifts Peter up. What a scene! As they enter the boat, the storm stops abruptly and the twelve leaders begin worshipping Jesus and saying, *"'Truly you are the Son of God'"* (Matt. 14:33). Now, I imagine some were jumping up and down and dancing and others were lying facedown worshipping. But there was one who was worshipping at a totally different level than the others. I imagine Peter, the one who had not only experienced the storm stopping, but had also walked on water, experienced a different level of worship. He was the only other person, outside of Jesus, to ever walk on water! His praise must have been a bit sweeter, having taken the step of faith to get out of the boat and obeying Jesus in faith.

Water Walker

"He saw the disciples straining at the oars, because the wind was against them. About the fourth watch of the night he went out to them, walking on the lake."

Mark 6:48

Personal Notes

SEEING GOD

Live It Out

Well, are you a water-walker or boat-hugger? The only way you can "walk on water" as a leader is to keep your eyes on Jesus. He is the author, leader and perfecter of your faith. Become consumed by Him, taking every thought captive to the obedience of Jesus. Consider where you may need to take a step of faith in your life. What is your next step of faith? Have a good discussion with your disciples today about being water-walkers or boat-huggers.

Other Thoughts

Digging Deeper

Psalms 145:14-16

2 Corinthians 10:5

Philippians 2:5-11

Titus 2:11-14

Hebrews 11:6

Hebrews 12:1-3

DAY 37 | Retreat and Evaluation

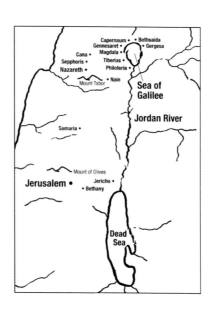

After walking on water, Jesus continues to train His leadership team for the mission. He is teaching them about love, humility, faith and their understanding of authority. He will cast out various demons, heal a little girl, confront the religious leaders once again and feed 4,000 people, a similar miracle because *"they had not understood about the loaves; their hearts were hardened"* (Mark 6:52). It is time now for another retreat with His leadership team, so He takes them north to the district of Caesarea Philippi (Matt. 16:13). Check out what happens next!

Read: Matthew 16:13-28; Mark 8:27-38; Luke 9:18-27.

What do you know about Caesarea Philippi?

What were people saying about Jesus?

What declaration did Peter make about Jesus? How did Jesus then respond?

Jesus then revealed some new things (Matt. 16:19,21). In this context, what was Jesus trying to teach His disciples?

What other questions do you still have?

Son of the Living God

"Simon Peter answered, 'You are the Christ, the Son of the living God.'"

Matthew 16:16

Personal Notes

Outside the Box

Jesus moves north with His leaders for some time away from the crowds, for a ministry team retreat. As they make their way north, Jesus begins evaluating the ministry with them. He asks them a simple question that sparks an incredible declaration. The question: *"'Who do people say I am?'"* (Mark 8:27). It is the most important question the leadership team can be asked. Notice the question is not about how many people are involved in the ministry. It is not about how many new followers are there. It is a question that cuts to the core of the movement. The question is about what people actually know about Jesus and not about what people know about me, my group, my church, my life, my job, my friends or my organization. Can you see the big difference? In the humanistic, materialistic, self-centered world in which we find ourselves, the question of who Jesus is doesn't fit very well. There is no time for contemplating that question because we are all too consumed with who we are. In the eternal scope of things, the most important question you will ever answer is: Who is Jesus and what do we do with Him?

How would the disciples know what the people were thinking about Jesus? Remember, they had been involved in some heavy-duty, people-intensive ministry for the past six months. They went on a short term mission project, feeding 5,000 men, women and children. They were highly qualified to evaluate the general pulse of the people. The answer they gave must have been a bit discouraging for Jesus: *"'Some say John the Baptist; others say Elijah; and, still others, Jeremiah or one of the prophets'"* (Matt. 16:14). After almost three years of public ministry, telling people that He was fully God, the Messiah, fully human, born in Bethlehem, schooled in Egypt and raised in Nazareth, and they only think He is John, Elijah, Jeremiah or some prophet. Can you hear the discouragement in Jesus' voice and feel His pain as He responds to their evaluation of the movement by asking them, *"'But what about you? Who do you say I am?'"* (Matt. 16:15). He may have been almost wincing, not sure He wanted to hear the answer. I think the disciples huddled for a while; then returned with this incredible answer spoken by the oldest leader, Peter: *"You are the Christ, the Son of the living God"* (Matt.16:16). Wow! What an unbelievable response by His leaders! They had it right! They figured it out; they were learning and growing in their knowledge of who He was. Inside, Jesus must have taken courage that everything He had done up until this point by investing in them was not in vain. Peter sees Jesus' pleasure and everyone starts to pat Peter on the back, "Good answer, good answer!" Jesus sees that they are proud of their accomplishment and seizes the moment to teach yet another important leadership principle. Jesus basically says, "Simon Peter, you know that your earthly dad did not reveal this truth to you, so don't take even a moment to bathe in your human pride. My Father in heaven revealed the truth to you" (Matt. 16:17).

We saw this principle back in John 3 when we had an encounter with John the Baptist at the river Aenon. Remember, John, the humble leader, said, *"'A man can receive only what is given him from heaven'"* and *"'He must become greater; I must become less'"* (John 3:27,30). If you understand anything about Jesus, it is because God has been gracious to you and revealed this truth to you. It is not because you are more intelligent or smarter than anyone else. It is solely because God, in His grace, willingly chose to reveal that to you. If you are learning anything from this study, it is not because I am some great writer of devotional material. It is because your Father in heaven has been gracious to you and has opened your understanding and revealed His Son to you. There is no place for boasting from creatures who are 100 percent dependent on a greater power, a divine being so much bigger than ourselves. All we can do is fall on our knees and say, "Thank you, thank you, thank you. I am not worthy, and yet you loved me enough to open my eyes and reveal your Son, Jesus, to me and save me. I worship you."

Live It Out

I do not want to pass up this opportunity to correct two teachings that the Christian Church has used for centuries which have caused enormous problems, division and pain. The problem revolves around what Jesus says in this passage, *"'And I tell you that you are Peter, and on this rock I will build my church, and the gates of Hades will not overcome it"* (Matt. 16:18). Many have wrongly interpreted this to mean that Jesus was saying to Peter that He was going to build His Church on Peter, the rock. This could not be further from the truth. Paul makes it abundantly clear that Jesus is the rock (1 Cor. 10:4), the foundation (1 Cor. 3:11), and the cornerstone (Eph. 2:20) of the church. The thought that Peter was the rock has existed in certain parts of Christendom for so long because it was believed that the name, Peter, means "rock" (John 1:42). It does not — it means "stone." If there is any doubt, one need only to go to the words of Peter himself in 1 Peter 2:4 and see that Peter calls himself and us living stones build upon the cornerstone — who is Christ.

The other wrong teaching is that we are to separate ourselves from the world, to hunker down behind closed doors because the Kingdom of Darkness is advancing against us. The truth is that this verse teaches just the opposite. We are on the offensive, not the defensive. The gates of Hell cannot stand against the onslaught and attack of Jesus' Church. Let me make it really clear what this passage is teaching. The Church of Jesus Christ is built on Jesus as the bedrock, the foundation and the cornerstone. His Church has one head and that is Himself (Eph. 5:23). No man could even come close to leading the worldwide, multicultural, multigenerational, diverse Church of our Savior. Furthermore, Hell does not stand a chance against the advancement of the Church of Jesus Christ, not because we are some great army, but because the one out in front leading the charge is none other than the Lion of Judah, the King of Kings and Lord of Lords, who was and is and is to come. Spend some time asking God to help you put Jesus in His rightful place at the center of your life. Talk with your disciples today about these truths.

Other Thoughts

Digging Deeper

Matthew 7:21-27

Luke 6:46-49

1 Corinthians 10:1-5

1 Corinthians 3:11-23

Ephesians 2:17-22

1 Peter 2:4-12

Hebrews 11:10

DAY 38 | Multiplication by Reduction

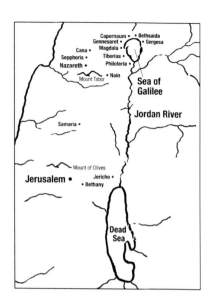

Six days after this incredible leadership team evaluation, Jesus reveals that He has begun a movement that is so powerful that the gates of Hell will not be able to slow its advance. Jesus, as the leader of this movement, is Himself the Lion of Judah and will lead the charge through the centuries. As they walk, He reveals to them that this advancement of the movement would not be without great personal suffering and loss of life (Matt. 16:21). Jesus then makes a bold move. Take a look!

Read: Matthew 17:1-13; Mark 9:2-13; Luke 9:28-36.

As you read about this event, list what you believe are some of the major details.

What is Jesus modeling for us about leadership by taking these three leaders with Him on a long journey to the mountains?

Why would this event follow the statement by Jesus that He "must go to Jerusalem" (Matt. 16:21)?

What other questions do you still have?

Outside the Box

Son of the Most High

"He will be great and will be called the Son of the Most High."

Luke 1:32

Personal Notes

Jesus is at another crucial point in the ministry. He knows the movement is expanding rapidly, and He needs help with the next steps. The first thing He does is choose three of the twelve leaders and calls them apart. Can you imagine the looks on the faces of the other nine as Jesus says to three of them, *"Come with Me."* Jesus will now be escaping regularly with His new "leaders of leaders." He knows that for the movement to grow He will have to have a few pillars on which to continue the construction (Gal. 2:9). He calls Peter, James and John to come even closer so that He may reveal more of who He is and give them some special instruction as the leaders of the leaders. With this in mind, they head up a mountain. Some people believe it was Mount Tabor, just outside of Nazareth, were Jesus had grown up. Others believe it was on Mount Hermon, north of Caesarea Philippi. I can only imagine the times Jesus had climbed this mountain and cried out to His Father through the years, especially in His youth — crying out to God to reveal Himself to Him, weeping and fasting for salvation to come to His people (Psa. 69:10). Something to take note of for those who live in the flatlands of this earth — when Scripture says Jesus went up the mountain, it is saying that He literally went up the mountain. Jesus was a climber, and if you have ever had the opportunity to be in Israel, you will know what I am talking about. Jesus had two places to escape the massive crowds of people circling Him at any given time: one was the quiet of the Sea of Galilee, the other was the top of the many different mountains around Israel.

Here on this mountain, something supernatural takes place. Can you imagine having this incredible opportunity to be present when Jesus is transfigured with His face and clothes shining bright (Matt. 17:2)? And then, out of nowhere, Moses and Elijah appear. By the way, how did they know the two guys that appeared with Jesus were Moses and Elijah? The only guess I can make is that Jesus must have introduced Moses and Elijah to His new leaders of leaders: "Hey, Peter, come here. I want to introduce you to two of my creations from a long time ago, Moses and Elijah. I know you have heard Me tell of them. Now come meet them." I can imagine the honor it was to stand in the presence of greatness — the greatest Old Testament leader, Moses, and the greatest Old Testament prophet, Elijah. Peter was impressed, so impressed that he opens his mouth, only to reveal how much he still needs to grow. He says, *"'If you wish, I will put up three shelters — one for you, one for Moses and one for Elijah'"* (Matt. 17:4). The Father cannot take Peter's lack of respect anymore. God hates idol worship (Deut. 16:22). He appears in a bright cloud and says, *"'This is my Son, whom love; with him I am well pleased. Listen to him!'"* (Matt. 17:5). He wanted Peter to know Moses and Elijah are not even close to Jesus in status, so not to insult Him any more by putting them on a pedestal along with the Son. No altars should be built to mere men. Peter had good intentions, but he just wasn't thinking before he said something.

Peter was caught up in the hero worship of his day, and forgot something he knew — that Jesus was the Son of the living God and that Moses and Elijah were not. Peter, James and John had been brought up in a Jewish culture that worshipped Moses and Elijah and had placed them on a pedestal, as if they were gods. When the three leaders heard the voice of God, they fell facedown, terrified. Jesus reaches down and says, "It's okay. Get up. It is just My Father, who is a bit frustrated with your lack of understanding and your misplaced hero-worship." But don't miss the fact that Peter, James and John all got to hear the audible voice of God, which only a few people in the history of the world have had the privilege to hear — people like Moses (Exod. 3:1-4:17) and Elijah (1 Kin. 19:11-18). Wow! God repeats the same thing he had said some three years earlier at the

Jordan River when John baptizes Jesus. Remember, Jesus came out of the water and prayed and the heavens opened. A dove descended and the voice of God said, *"'This is my Son, whom I love; with him I am well pleased'"* (Matthew 3:17).

Live It Out

As they come down off the mountain, Jesus instructs His leaders to not tell anyone of the visit until he rises from the dead. I am still left wondering: What was Jesus talking about with Moses and Elijah? (See Luke 9:31 for some insight.) Why did Jesus need to meet with them that day? And why was it so important that Peter, James and John be present? I certainly do not have all the answers; as you can tell by this study. I have many more questions than I have answers. However, I have learned from this event to not put people, even great leaders, on a pedestal. Even as leaders, we are very prone to hero-worship. In Christianity, we have many heroes, old and new, people who bring us the Word of God in terms that we connect with. Many of our heroes are Christian musicians, pastors, Bible teachers, Bible scholars, radio and TV personalities. Many are really good people, but not even close to Jesus. It grieves my heart as a leader of leaders to see so many Christians worshiping other people and not Jesus. The lack of knowledge of who Jesus is is very discouraging to me, and the reason I wrote this study was to help people know that there is only One, and His name is Jesus.

I am sorry, world, but I already have a hero and His name is Jesus! No American Idol, Latin American Idol, no idol-worship here, just worshiping and adoring Jesus. Spend a few moments examining your own life for any idols lurking in the closets. Listen to the voice of the Father and clean house. Talk with your disciple today about this theme of idol-worship. Remember, God will not share your worship with any others.

Other Thoughts

Digging Deeper

Exodus 3:1 - 4:17

1 Kings 19:11-18

1 Samuel 3:1-21

Psalms 46:9-10

SEEING GOD

DAY 39 | Leadership and Compassion

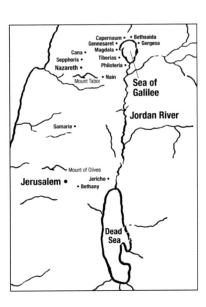

After meeting with Moses and Elijah, they went back down the mountain and *"[w]hen they came back to the other disciples, they saw a large crowd around them and the teachers of the law arguing with them. As soon as all the people saw Jesus, they were overwhelmed with wonder and ran to greet him"* (Mark 9:14-15). Jesus comes down off the mountain and is immediately confronted with the needs of the people. He ministers to the people as the movement continues to expand. I wonder what will happen this year at the feast? Check it out!

Read: John 7:1-8:11.

Go through this passage and list all of the questions raised by various people. (I counted almost 20.)

What were the various views presented about who Jesus is? (I counted at least 12.)

What does this tell us about the crowds?

What does this tell us about Jesus?

What leadership lessons can we learn from this?

What other questions do you still have?

Outside the Box

The Bible says that the Jewish holiday, the Feast of the Tabernacles was coming up (John 7:2). It was at that time of the year when all Jewish men must report to Jerusalem and present themselves at the Feast of Tabernacles, an Old Testament mandated seven-day men's retreat each year. (If you want to read more about it check out Leviticus 23:33-36 and Deuteronomy 16:13-17.) Jesus' half-brothers (half-brothers because they had the same mom but not the same dad), James, Joseph, Judas and Simon were really excited about making this yearly pilgrimage with their older brother, Jesus. Yet they were still struggling to believe that He was not only the brother they had known their whole lives, but also the Messiah *"[f]or even his own brothers did not believe in him"* (John 7:5). We are not sure when Jesus' half brothers become Christ-followers but somewhere along the way at least two of them, James and Judas, do. We know this because we have a book written by each of them — the books James and Jude. We also know James becomes the first senior leader of the church in Jerusalem and was known as James the Lesser, or "camel knees," a name given to him because of his passion for praying on his knees around Jerusalem. Maybe the biggest thing James took away from living with Jesus some thirty years was Jesus' prayer life.

In obedience to the Father, Jesus tells His brothers to go without Him to the feast, which must have sounded odd to them. But they listened and headed off to Jerusalem. Obviously, the Father wanted some time alone with Jesus to talk and then sent Him into Jerusalem undercover. Midway through the feast, Jesus makes His grand appearance at the temple and begins to teach once again about who He is, that He was born in Bethlehem, a son of David, yet raised in Nazareth. (Maybe this is when His brothers become believers. Who knows?) A fight breaks out among the crowd, because of what Jesus is saying and what the people had been taught about the Messiah. There is a fight, a lot of yelling, and Jesus just slips away to the quiet of the Mount of Olives to spend some time with His Father again. This small mount was obviously His favorite spot to pray when He was in Jerusalem. Meanwhile, the religious crowd is fighting as well, and who takes a stand for Jesus but good old Nicodemus! Remember him? He was the guy who came to Jesus at night back in John 3. Nicodemus gets his chance to stand up for Jesus. He makes a calculated risk and decides to ask those gathered a question. Instead of changing minds, he is verbally attacked and ridiculed, accused of being from Galilee as well. Nicodemus recoils and goes back into hiding and continues to be a true believer, a Christ-follower, but not yet a

Personal Notes

SEEING GOD

fully committed disciple. We will keep an eye on this Christ-follower, who is somewhat undercover among the religious crowd of Jesus' day. Do you know any undercover Christians? The kind who says their relationship is something personal and meant to be kept in the privacy of their own thoughts and life? Are you a secret follower?

When Jesus came back from the Mount of Olives, a woman is brought before Him, who had committed adultery. If this was a gathering exclusively of men, what was this woman doing there? And where is the man who was caught in adultery with her? Was he not just as guilty? Why is he not presented as well before Jesus? Why only the woman? I smell a rat. I think a plan had been hatched the night before and it is about to backfire in the faces of those who planned it. The scribes and the Pharisees have heard that Jesus is a friend of sinners and seize the opportunity to use this against Him. They bring this woman, who I am sure is scared to death, and place her in the center of the court, quote the law of Moses to Him and then ask Him, "What do you think needs to be done with her?"

Live It Out

This was obviously a trap, because if Jesus said to stone her, He would be cheered as a law keeper, but when word spread throughout the land, every prostitute and sinner would run from Jesus. It is interesting that in Jesus' day prostitutes and sinners ran to Jesus for grace and forgiveness and today most prostitutes and sinners run as far away from the church of Jesus Christ as they can get. What's that about? If you ask them, you will find that they anticipate condemnation and not love, forgiveness and grace. Where have we gone wrong?

Jesus sniffs out the plot to trap Him and turns the tables. Standing next to the woman, He begins to write in the dirt. I wonder what He wrote. Through the centuries, Christians have debated what Jesus wrote in the sand. Some say He drew the early Christian symbol of a fish. It sounds cool, but it says He wrote something, not drew something. My best guess is that He wrote the Ten Commandments that Moses had given the people, which the religious elders were quoting from when they brought the woman to Jesus. He makes them think back to His teaching from the day before: *"Has not Moses given you the law? Yet not one of you keeps the law"* (John 7:19). They persist and refuse to get the point, so He stands up and says, *"If any one of you is without sin, let him be the first to throw a stone at her"* (John 8:7). Then notice what Jesus does. He doesn't back up or run away, he stays there right beside the woman and continues to write. Maybe He was now writing out their sins: lying, deception, gossip, back-biting, taking vengeance, etc. As Jesus continues to write, the crowd disperses, beginning with the oldest. Not one person threw a stone at her. When all have left Jesus stands up again and says, *"Then neither do I condemn you. Go now and leave your life of sin"* (John 8:11). We can always look to Jesus, *"... for his compassions never fail. They are new every morning; great is your faithfulness"* (Lam. 3:22-23). Leading with compassion, imitating God the Father, letting Jesus live through you — that is my prayer for you today. Talk with your disciple today about leadership with compassion.

Other Thoughts

Digging Deeper

Deuteronomy 4:31

Nehemiah 9:17-19

Psalms 72:13

Lamentations 3:22-23

Joel 2:12-13

Romans 8:1-11

Colossians 3:12-17

DAY 40 | Jesus, Light of the World

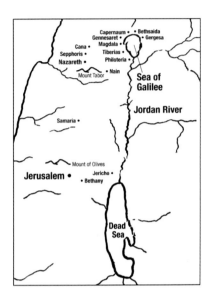

Jesus returns to the Galilee and continues to train His apostles and prepare the next group of disciples who He will soon send out on their first mission trip. But there is another feast, the Feast of Dedication, or Lights. This is not an Old Testament feast, but a new one added several years before Jesus comes on the scene. This was in honor of the miracle that took place when God supernaturally provided light in the lamps when there was not enough oil to keep them burning, when the temple was taken back during the Jewish Maccabees' revolt under the leadership of Judas Maccabees. What will happen on this next trip to Jerusalem? Who will Jesus meet and what trap will the religious leaders set for Him? Read on!

Read: John 9:1-41.

What would it be like to be blind from birth? As a blind person, what would it be like to hear this conversation near you?

Trace the progression of the blind man receiving sight.

v. 1

v. 11

v. 17

v. 27

v .33

v. 38

Trace the progression of the Pharisees becoming blind.

v. 15

v. 16

v. 24

vs. 28-29

v. 34

v. 39

What lessons can we learn from this story?

What other questions do you still have?

The Light
of the World

"'While I am in the
world, I am the light
of the world.'"

John 9:5

Personal Notes

Outside the Box

As Jesus is on His way to the Feast of Lights with a multitude of disciples, they pass by a man who they later find out was blind from birth. It was the belief at that time that if someone was suffering, it was because they or someone close to them had sinned. This is still a commonly-held belief throughout the world and in the Christian church. In fact, in Chicago where I grew up, I was taught by culture that suffering was a bad thing and being poor was a curse. Poverty and suffering were things to run from, protect yourself against and make sure you went through as little as possible. The belief was that **all** poverty and suffering were due to the poor choices one makes in life and the fault of one's own inability to get motivated and go to work. It is still hard for me to shake this humanistic teaching. It is true that we all experience suffering and poverty because of bad choices we have made, but there are other reasons why God lets us go through suffering. If you have not been there yet, you will be. Trust me. It is part of the human experience.

I can understand suffering for bad choices, but what about when you suffer innocently? What then? Why do good people suffer through hard times that are not deserved? Why are babies born blind? Why do innocent children suffer at the hands of abusive parents? Jesus answers these questions in this passage, but be warned — it may seriously change your viewpoint and cause you to wrestle with the justice issues in your own life.

The disciples questioned Jesus, "'*Rabbi, who sinned, this man or his parents, that he was born blind?*'" (John 9:2). They knew sin caused suffering in peoples' lives. What is shocking is Jesus response to their question by saying that, "'*[n]either this man nor his parents sinned*'" (John 9:3). Sometimes people suffer for reasons other than poor choices and the sin of others. Jesus says this man was born blind just "'*so that the work of God might be displayed in his life*'" (John 9:3). In other words, this thirty-some-year-old man was born blind so that, on this day, Jesus could walk by and declare Himself to be the Light of the World and open his eyes to the glory of the Father. It is so hard to get my mind around this concept, that God would allow someone to suffer so that He might be glorified. I am so me-centered that I think the world revolves around me, my family and my friends. I struggle to understand how a good God would allow evil and suffering to exist. The problem is not God's; the problem is mine. I think God exists for me when, in reality, I exist for Him. He is the center and not me. What is happening in our world will ultimately bring Him honor and glory, because it is all about Him and not about me. I so want it to be about me, but the truth is that no matter how much I try to make it about me, it is still about Him. He alone sits enthroned on high (Psa. 113:5).

SEEING GOD

My world says that poor people are cursed and that poverty is something to avoid at all costs. And yet my Jesus says blessed are the poor (Luke 6:20) and that all those who will live godly lives in Christ Jesus will suffer (2 Tim. 3:12). Poverty and suffering come into our lives so that God will ultimately get the glory as He saves the day. How could He be the Savior that He is if we did not need Him to save the day? Poverty and suffering come into the life of the disciple because they are tools in the hand of the Father to conform me into the image of Jesus (Rom. 8:29). Another leadership lesson is to be careful about judging why someone is suffering. It could be that they have not sinned, made a bad choice or failed to look ahead — it may just be that they suffer so that God will get the glory when He delivers them from their suffering.

Live It Out

These are tough truths, I know. I find it so hard to accept that the world does not revolve around me and that I am not in control of my environment. I cannot eliminate all the suffering of those around me. If I could eliminate world hunger and world suffering, I would do it in a moment. I hate to see people suffer. I wish I could just take the suffering from them. But I know that God has a purpose for the suffering we go through. It is to make us more like Jesus. Spend some time today talking with someone about suffering and poverty. Ask God to open your eyes to His plans and His ways. Be careful to not sit in the seat of judgment. God is the only one who sees all and knows all. He alone can judge what is just and unjust.

Other Thoughts

Digging Deeper

Luke 6:22-23

Romans 8:18

Philippians 3:10

Colossians 1:24

2 Timothy 1:8

2 Timothy 2:2-13

2 Timothy 3:12

Hebrews 12:1-3

1 Peter 2:21

1 Peter 4:13

DAY 41 | Leadership Multiplication

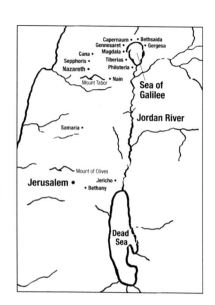

Jesus leaves the Feast of Dedication and travels to the other side of the Jordan River, where John had baptized him three years earlier (John 10:40). Jesus will use this as a base for the next few months, awaiting His final entrance into Jerusalem and His pending death on the cross. What will He do in these last several months to ensure that the movement continues after He is taken up to His Father? What will His final steps be? Let's look in on what this passage says.

Read: Luke 10:1-42.

What are Jesus' priorities in this passage?

In what ways could Jesus have been distracted from these priorities (like Martha in v. 40)?

Why does Jesus so greatly rejoice in Luke 10:21?

What do you see as the primary lessons in this passage?

What other questions do you still have?

The Door

"Therefore Jesus said again, I tell you the truth, 'I am the gate for the sheep.'"

John 10:7

Personal Notes

Outside the Box

As the movement continues to grow, Jesus assembles the next set of leaders and appoints them in much the same way as He had with the twelve. They were obviously disciples who had given up everything to follow Him, and were now ready to be part of the growing leadership team. He calls them together, gives them some final instructions and sends them on their way ahead of Him into the last district to be reached — Perea. Why does Jesus send them out with nothing?

Remember what we learned as to why He sent the first twelve out with nothing? Jesus knows His time is short and He wants them to learn to be dependent on the Father. He wants them to see that if they will only step out in faith, God will go before them and provide everything they need to complete the mission He has called them to. He wants these new leaders to learn to walk by faith and not by sight.

They move out as a great army of evangelists into the harvest fields of Perea. They are to go to the village, find the man of peace, stay and minister out of that house, healing the sick and telling them about the coming kingdom of God. If the village doesn't receive them, leave peaceably and shake the dust off their feet and continue to proclaim that *"'the kingdom of God is near'"* (Luke 10:11).

They return from their mission trip jumping up and down, saying, *"'Lord, even the demons submit to us in your name'"* (Luke 10:17). At this, Jesus seizes an opportunity to say, *"'... do not rejoice that the spirits submit to you, but rejoice that your names are written in heaven'"* (Luke 10:20). In other words, don't get excited about the demons obeying you; instead, get excited about the fact that your names are written in the Book of Life along with the new people who have entered the Kingdom due to the work of God. Don't get more excited about the temporal than about the spiritual. Lives and destinies were changed on your trip — rejoice in that.

Jesus then breaks into spontaneous praise to His Father, and with great joy in His heart, He begins to worship the Father, *"'I praise you, Father, Lord of heaven and earth, because you have hidden these things from the wise and learned, and revealed them to little children. Yes, Father, for this was your good pleasure'"* (Luke 10:21). Jesus is so excited! But why? Why is Jesus so overjoyed at this point? What causes Jesus to rejoice so greatly? I think the key is that He knows that God has been well pleased with His work. The plan is working and the disciples have been made into men with passion and heart to tell others the good news. The will of the Father was that Jesus would die on the cross, but the work of the Father was that Jesus would make disciples, who could make disciples, who could make disciples. Jesus sees that the way of the Father will bring glory to Him. This was Jesus' passion, that the Father would be glorified. And it was happening in front of His very eyes. His work was coming to a close and this work of making disciples who could make disciples was going to change the planet.

Live It Out

There is a joy that comes when you personally watch someone you have shared with come to Christ. It is incredible to watch the transformation with your own eyes. Yet, there is a joy that is deeper, the joy of watching someone you have poured your life into, share Jesus with someone and seeing that person come to Christ. It is the joy of multiplication. Now there are two of you who are glorifying the Father, living in obedience to His will, dying to self and doing His work of making disciples. Have you experienced these two joys? If not, what is stopping you? Spend some time with your disciples talking about the joy of multiplication.

Other Thoughts

Digging Deeper

Psalms 69:28

Philippians 4:3-4

Revelation 13:8

Revelation 17:8

Revelation 20:15

Revelation 21:27

SEEING GOD

DAY 42 | Unleavened Leadership

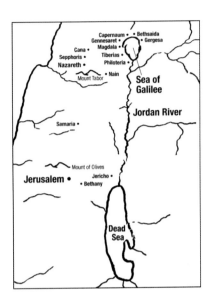

Jesus continues His teaching over the next several months. We only have time in this study to cover a couple of His lessons on leadership development. These days for Jesus are packed with incredible teaching on the development of leaders. One of the most important teachings that Jesus gives during this time is on being an unleavened leader. Read carefully and digest what Jesus is saying to His disciples about leadership. He is calling for a radically different style of leadership than what they had seen their whole lives from the religious leaders. As you read, ask God to examine your leadership style.

Read: Luke 12:1-12; Matthew 16:1-12.

What is hypocrisy — how would you define it?

List all the results of hypocrisy found in Matthew 23:13-35.

What was the leaven, the yeast, of the leadership in Israel (Luke 12:1; Matt. 16:12)?

What type of hypocrisy did the disciples need to fear?

How do you find hypocrisy creeping into your life?

What other questions do you still have?

Outside the Box

During the past six months, Jesus has been continually drawing a sharp distinction between the type of leadership He expects and the type of leadership His disciples have had as a model growing up in Israel. He does this by stopping periodically and pointing out that how the leaders of Israel are leading is not in keeping with the leadership Jesus desires of them. Jesus says that there is something in the Jewish leaders of His day that causes them to lead poorly. They have been corrupted, and that corruption is leaven, or yeast. Leaven is an ingredient that people would add to bread or wine to give it body. You simply put in a small amount of yeast into the bread or wine and in a short time it affects the whole thing, changing it.

In the Old Testament, God told the people to search their homes and throw out any leaven and then make unleavened bread to eat for seven days. This dates all the way back to the exodus from Egypt (Exod. 12:14-20). On the night before the Israelites were to leave Egypt, Moses commands the people: *"'For seven days you are to eat bread made without yeast. On the first day remove the yeast from your house ...'"* (Exod. 12:15). Leaven, or yeast, in the Old Testament was a symbol of sin.

Jesus takes this common practice in Israel and uses it as a teaching illustration for His young leaders. He knew it would be something that they would always remember because it was sewn into the fabric of their culture. Jesus says that there are two different types of leaven that they, as true disciples, should beware of, two ingredients in poor leadership that they should watch out for and purge from their leadership style, so that they might be unleavened bread (1 Cor. 5:8). He directs, *"'Be on your guard against the yeast of the Pharisees and Sadducees'"* (Matt. 16:6). The two types of leaven to guard against are the leaven of the Pharisees and the leaven of the Sadducees.

Jesus tells us that the leaven of the Pharisees is their hypocrisy (Luke 12:1). They taught one thing and lived another. Beware, young leader, of the leaven of the Pharisee. You should practice what you preach. If you tell people they need to be involved in making disciples, then you need to be making disciples as well. I have met many who give lip service to the Great Commission and the making of disciples. They talk a great game, but when you ask them about their disciples, they have all kinds of excuses for why they are not actively, intentionally investing their lives in others. Beware of a lifestyle that demonstrates something other than what you are teaching.

The leaven of the Sadducees can be seen best in another book that was written by Luke: *"The Sadducees say that there is no resurrection, and that there are neither angels nor spirits"* (Acts 23:8). Jesus had been teaching that there are two resurrections, where *"' those who have done good will rise to live, and those who have done evil will rise to be condemned'"* (John 5:29). He goes on to say, *"'I am the resurrection and the*

Bread of Life

"Then Jesus declared, 'I am the bread of life. He who comes to me will never go hungry, and he who believes in me will never be thirsty.'"

John 6:35

Personal Notes

SEEING GOD

life'" (John 11:25). The leaven of the Sadducees was that they hardened their hearts to the truth. They were more interested in being right than in what was really the truth. Beware, young leader, of the leaven of the Sadducees. Do not harden your heart. Remain teachable and open to be transformed by the truth. Don't think you know it all — stay teachable and willing to be transformed by the truth you have yet to discover about God. Don't put God in a box and think you have it all figured out. There are many truths that God still longs for you to know about Him and His Son. In fact, that is the reason for eternity: *"'Now this is eternal life: that they may know you, the only true God, and Jesus Christ, whom you have sent'"* (John 17:3). Let God the Father continue His work in you. Get rid of all the pride and humble yourself before the Father.

Live It Out

Both groups of leaders, the Pharisees and the Sadducees, had been corrupted by the world around them. They lacked sincerity and would not believe the truth. Paul says, *"Therefore let us keep the Festival, not with the old yeast, the yeast of malice and wickedness, but with bread without yeast, the bread of sincerity and truth."* (1 Cor. 5:8). Beware, young leader, of the leaven of hypocrisy, insincerity and hard-heartedness.

It does not take much leaven to infect your whole life and wound those around you. Just a little pride, hypocrisy, insincerity and an immobile heart will affect the world around you. Discuss with your disciple today these cautions for a leader. How does one know if they have leaven in their life? How do you clean house of all the leaven? Think about it.

Other Thoughts

Digging Deeper

Exodus 12:14-20

Ezekiel 34:1-31

Mark 8:11-21

Acts 23:6-10

1 Corinthians 5:6-8

DAY 43 | Leadership is Stewardship

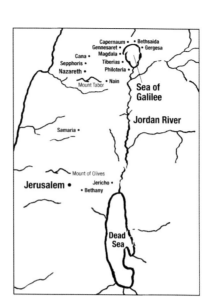

After spending several months on the other side of the Jordan River in Perea, Jesus makes His way back across the Jordan and into the town of Jericho, where He will reinforce many of the leadership principles that He has been teaching His growing team of leaders. He will live them out and put them into practice once again. Jesus was a person who did not just talk about things, but actually acted on them. He so desires to live out these principles through you and me today, if we will only yield to Him. Check out Jesus in action, living out what He teaches, unlike the Pharisees.

Read: Luke 19:1-27.

What do you know about Jericho?

What do we know about Zacchaeus from this passage?

What lessons can we learn from the Zacchaeus experience?

Why do you think Jesus told this parable of a certain nobleman in Luke 19:11-27?

What are major life lessons that we can get from this parable?

What other questions do you still have?

Pearl of Great Value

"'When he found one of great value, he went away and sold everything he had and bought it.'"

Matthew 13:46

Personal Notes

Outside the Box

In Jericho, Jesus meets another very rich man, who is the chief tax collector of the region for Rome. He mostly likely knows Matthew and maybe even is a good friend. It is also possible that Zacchaeus had been one of the many tax collectors that Matthew had invited to his house to meet Jesus (Luke 5:29). It is interesting that when Jesus sees Zacchaeus up in the tree, He calls him by name. How did Jesus know his name? Maybe Matthew had frequently talked about the short, chief tax collector who lived in Jericho. Jesus goes to Zacchaeus' home and he becomes a believer and the Savior saves him from himself. Zacchaeus is so overjoyed at the forgiveness he receives that he does what all true believers do — he asks for forgiveness and makes things right with those they have hurt in life. It is on this note that Jesus begins His final walk to Jerusalem. And even though Jesus had made it clear many times that He was going to Jerusalem to suffer at the hands of the religious leaders, His followers must not have wanted to believe this truth. In their defense, everything around them shouted that this would not happen. The movement had grown large and multitudes of people were following Jesus. He had a large crowd of committed disciples all descending on Jerusalem for the Passover.

As Jesus walks along listening to the disciples chatting (no doubt about what they had just seen — a rich person giving his wealth to the poor), Jesus realizes that they think that the kingdom of God is going to appear immediately. They do not understand that He is really going to die and leave them for a period of time. Jesus decides to give them a parable to help them understand that there will be a period of time in which they will be entrusted with the message of the Gospel and that they are to be good stewards of this message.

Let me try to unwrap this parable for you. We have several characters. There is the nobleman (Jesus), who comes from a faraway place (heaven) to redeem His rightful kingdom. So he calls ten slaves and gives them each one mina (three-and-a-half months wages), and he tells them to do business with the mina until he returns. The nobleman expected these ten slaves to get busy and multiply the mina that he has entrusted to them. But many of the citizens of the land did not want the nobleman to reign over them, just like many of the citizens of this world do not want Jesus to reign over them. So they send a delegation to tell the nobleman just that. He was made king, however, and then returns. Upon returning now as king, he calls the slaves to give an account of how they have used the mina entrusted to them. One by one they appear before the King and give an account for what they have done with the investment he has made in them. The first says, *"'Sir, your mina has earned ten more'"* (Luke 19:16). The second says, *"'Sir, your mina has earned five more'"* (Luke 19:18). Note that these first two servants knew whose mina it was, they took their job seriously and went to work. They obeyed the master and received rewards proportionate to their faithfulness and ability to multiply what the master had given them.

Another servant appears before the Master with nothing but excuses, and pretty lame ones at that. He had not obeyed and multiplied the investment made by the Master in him. The Master is very displeased with the disobedient and lazy slave and takes the one mina away from him and gives it to the one that had multiplied ten fold. Jesus' audience is furious and shouts, "That's not fair; that guy already has ten!" But Jesus replies, *"'I tell you that to everyone that has, more will be given, but as for the one who has nothing, even what he has will be taken away. But those enemies of mine who did not want me to be king over them — bring them here and kill them in front of me'"* (Luke 19:26-27).

Live It Out

The truths in verses 26 and 27 are ones we do not want to accept. They seem harsh, unloving and unfair. But they are not — in God's eyes, they are just, well deserved and more than fair. I will leave you to struggle with the truth of God's word. Like me, you need a transformation of mind for your eyes to be opened. So I entrust you to the One who can transform your thinking — Jesus (Rom. 12:1-2).

We are stewards of the mysteries or the hidden things, Paul says. We are stewards of not just material things but of spiritual things. God is teaching you things about Jesus that are to be passed on. They are being entrusted to you through this study of Jesus' life and now you must to pass them on. May God help you to be faithful in this assignment. The disciple of Jesus owns nothing but is a steward of everything His Father gives him charge over. And each of us will be held accountable for what he has been called to steward: our time, our words, our thoughts and our actions. Take some time to talk with your disciple today about the concept of stewardship.

Other Thoughts

Digging Deeper

Matthew 25:14-30

1 Corinthians 3:12-15

1 Corinthians 4:1-2

1 Corinthians 9:16-18

Ephesians 3:1-21

Colossians 1:24-29

DAY 44 | Passionate Leadership

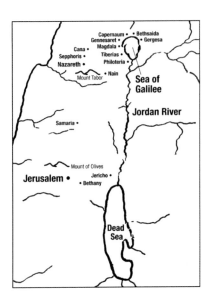

As Jesus makes His way from Jericho to Jerusalem, He is about to receive an incredible gift from the Father — a king's welcome into the Holy City. It is a day of celebration and great emotion. What will happen as Jesus enters into Jerusalem? Take a close look!

Read: Luke 19:28-48; Matthew 21:1-17; Mark 11:1-26; John 12:12-19.

As you study these passages, how do you visualize the energy of this moment?

How did Jesus respond to these crowds?

What is the feeling as Jesus enters Jerusalem?

What are the different groups saying about Jesus?

What other questions do you still have?

Outside the Box

A prophecy given hundreds of years earlier is being fulfilled before these young leaders' eyes: *"Rejoice greatly, O Daughter of Zion! Shout, Daughter of Jerusalem! See, your king is coming to you, righteous and having salvation, gentle and riding on a donkey, on a colt, the foal of a donkey"* (Zech. 9:9). The King has arrived and shouts fill the air, *"'Blessed is the king who comes in the name of the Lord!' 'Peace in heaven and glory in the highest!'"* (Luke 19:38). Others shouted, *"'Hosanna!' 'Blessed is he who comes in the name of the Lord!' 'Blessed is the coming kingdom of our father David!' 'Hosanna in the highest!'"* (Mark 11:9-10). And still others, *"'Blessed is the King of Israel!'"* (John 12:13). All of these praises were filling the air! There was a line of people stretching from the entrance of Jerusalem to the descent of the Mount of Olives. There were so many thousands of people in this line that Pharisees were saying to each other, *"Look how the whole world has gone after him!"* (John 12:19). Of course, you know how the story ends. So how does a crowd of hundreds of thousands of people shout, *"Hosanna to the King of Israel!"* one day and change to *"Crucify Him!"* (John 19:15) only six days later? It's just amazing.

Don't miss what John adds to his description of the ride into the city. John says that he remembers as they approached the city, Jesus began to weep as he looked upon it. Then Jesus, just as He did three years ago, gives a prophecy. Last time the prophecy was about the temple of His body, this time the prophecy is about the physical temple and city of Jerusalem. Jesus says, *"They will dash you to the ground, you and the children within your walls. They will not leave one stone on another, because you did not recognize the time of God's coming to you"* (Luke 19:44). Jesus pronounces judgment on the city for their unbelief. This prophecy of Jesus came true in 70 AD when Titus destroyed the city of Jerusalem and tore down the temple and city walls.

Jesus parades into Jerusalem on a donkey. What an entrance for the King of Kings and the Lord of Lords! The people shout back, throwing their coats and cutting branches from the trees along the way and spreading them on the road. The Bible said that *"[w]hen Jesus entered Jerusalem, the whole city was stirred and asked, 'Who is this?' The crowds answered, 'This is Jesus, the prophet from Nazareth in Galilee'"* (Matt. 21:10-11). Jesus enters the temple and what does He see but the same scene from three years earlier. The people are again selling doves and exchanging money. Jesus responds in a similar fashion by driving them out of the temple and turning over the tables of the money changers. But this time He adds, *"'My house will be called a house of prayer,' but you are making it a 'den of robbers'"* (Matthew 21:13), quoting from two Old Testament passages, Isaiah 56:7 and Jeremiah 7:11. It is obvious from Jesus' response that they were taking advantage once again of the poor and the foreigners. The poor people were the ones buying doves because they can't afford to use lambs as sacrifices (Leviticus 5:7). The foreigners were the ones changing money, because they charged a poll tax to enter the temple and they would only take Jewish money. They did not want money with Caesar's picture on it, thus forcing those coming from great distances to exchange their money most likely at a poor exchange rate.

Son of David

"The crowds that went ahead of him and those that followed shouted, 'Hosanna to the Son of David!' 'Blessed is he who comes in the name of the Lord!' 'Hosanna in the highest!'"

Matthew 21:9

Personal Notes

SEEING GOD

The people had come seeking to pray and to worship the one true God, and others had chosen to seize the opportunity to take advantage of them. To make it worse, the two groups that they had chosen to take advantage of were the poor and the foreigners and, throughout the Old Testament, God had warned the people of taking advantage of these two groups.

Live It Out

Jesus responds passionately and deliberately by shutting down these businesses. Remember the last time He had done this, years earlier at the beginning of His ministry? Jesus had said, *"'Destroy this temple, and I will raise it again in three days'"* (John 2:19). Had they been listening? Jesus' own words are about to come true at this Passover, because Jesus is our Passover Lamb (1 Cor. 5:7). Lead with passion, but make sure your passion is in the right place. You need a passion for His name and His fame — not for yourself or some organization, no matter how great they may be. Spend some time talking to your disciples about having a passion as Jesus had.

Other Thoughts

Digging Deeper

Numbers 25:10-13

1 Kings 18:20-46; 19:10

John 2:13-25

2 Corinthians 11:21-33

DAY 45 | Servant Leadership

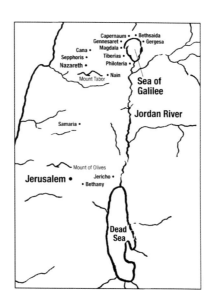

Jesus spends the week teaching at the temple during the day and in prayer, communicating to His Father each evening on the Mount of Olives (Luke 21:37). The things Jesus teaches this week are incredibly significant. They are a study, in and of themselves, full of leadership lessons and truths. The week is coming to a close, and Jesus' time is short, so He has a few of His disciples make arrangements for a Passover supper in town. Jesus has been eagerly anticipating and preparing for this particular evening. He says, *"'I have eagerly desired to eat this Passover with you before I suffer. For I tell you, I will not eat it again until it finds fulfillment in the kingdom of God'"* (Luke 22:15-16). What will happen on this last Passover night? Take a look.

Read: Luke 22:7-38; Matthew 26:17-29; Mark 14:12-25; John 13:1-38.

What does this passage (John 13:1-38) tell us that Jesus knew?

What is Jesus modeling for us about leadership?

Did the disciples understand what Jesus was doing? How were they viewing what He was doing?

What other questions do you still have?

Our Passover

"Get rid of the old yeast that you may be a new batch without yeast—as you really are. For Christ, our Passover lamb, has been sacrificed."

1 Corinthians 5:7

Personal Notes

Outside the Box

There is so much here that Jesus is modeling for us about leadership. It is a long night of last-minute instructions, encouragement, vision and expressions of love. John says that Jesus *"now showed them the full extent of his love"* (John 13:1). One of the biggest expressions of His love follows as Jesus gets up from the supper, lays aside His outer garments, takes a towel and wraps it around Himself. He takes the role of a servant and washes His leaders' feet. I am sure they are stunned and a little embarrassed. None of them had taken the role of a servant and washed the feet of those entering. This, of course, was a custom in Jesus' day, that when a person entered someone's home, they would have someone wash the dirt of the city streets off their guests' feet. Jesus takes the role of the servant and then says, *"'Now that I, your Lord and Teacher, have washed your feet, you also should wash one another's feet. I have set you an example that you should do as I have done for you'"* (John 13:14-15). Jesus leads the way for teachers to wash the feet of students, for leaders to wash the feet of those they are leading. Jesus couldn't be much clearer, could He? Wash one another's feet, humble yourselves, get down and serve one another. But it is so hard! It is much easier to tell people what to do than to serve them. Servant leadership is often seen as being weak. We think we will lose the respect of those we lead if we get on our knees and serve. It is true — some people will respond as Peter did, exclaiming, *"'...you shall never wash my feet'"* (John 13:8). Some do not want to see you humble yourself because they do not want to do the same. In their minds, it is better to all stick together so as not to feel convicted. But we do not wash each other's feet because is the "in" thing to do. We wash each other's feet because that is the model our Master left for us. For the true disciples of Jesus, there is only one model and that is Jesus. That is why we call ourselves Christians, mini-Christs, or better yet, people who allow Christ to live in and through us.

After washing their feet and explaining to them that this was an example he was expecting from them, Jesus returns to the table to eat His last Passover supper. Why the last supper? Because tomorrow, the Lamb of God, was to die as our Passover, one last sacrifice for all time (Heb. 10:1-10). As Jesus takes His place at the supper, He becomes deeply grieved and tells them that one of His inner core of leaders will be the one to betray Him. Already the plot has been hatched — Judas has become disillusioned with the movement. He had already struck a deal with the religious leaders to betray our Lord. Something strikes me as odd: Why do the other disciples not suspect Judas as the betrayer when he gets up and leaves the supper? John must have been asked this question later on, for he writes, *"Since Judas had charge of the money, some thought Jesus was telling him to buy what was needed for the Feast, or to give something to the poor"* (John 13:29). My thought is that maybe, of all the disciples, Judas was the least likely. After all, he must have been the most trusted one because he held the moneybox. It is obvious that when he leaves no one flinches. Another unseen guest at the supper was Satan: *"As soon as Judas took the bread, Satan entered into him"* (John 13:27). That means that Satan must have been hanging around and probably saw the foot washing, laughing in a corner, thinking that Jesus was a ridiculous kind of leader.

After Judas has left the room, the disciples started talking once again about which one of them was the greatest. Jesus' words cannot be clearer. Read them again in Luke 22:25-27. They are powerful words that you should never forget. A leader is the one who serves, not the one who bosses others around.

Live It Out

If you want to see what Peter learned about servant leadership go to 1 Peter 5:1-9. At this same time, Jesus seizes the moment to give His leaders a new commandment, one He has lived in front of them for three and a half years now: *"'A new commandment I give you: Love one another. As I have loved you, so you must love one another'"* (John 13:34). The model for how they were to love one another was Jesus Himself. Our model for how to love one another is also Jesus. Do what Jesus did; love as Jesus loved. He also adds, *"'By this all men will know that you are my disciples, if you love one another'"* (John 13:35). Wow! The hallmark of a true disciple is love. Paul puts it this way, *"And now these three remain: faith, hope and love. But the greatest of these is love"* (1 Cor. 13:13).

Love is the mark of the true Christ-follower, a love for God and others. Is love the mark of your life? Spend some time evaluating and asking God to fill you with love. Talk with your disciples about servant leadership, Jesus-style. What does that look like today? How do you practically wash others' feet in your culture?

Other Thoughts

Digging Deeper

Matthew 22:37-40

Romans 15:7

1 Corinthians 13:1-13

Galatians 6:2

Ephesians 4:32

Colossians 3:12-17

1 Peter 3:8-9

1 Peter 5:1-7

SEEING GOD

DAY 46 | Submissive Leadership

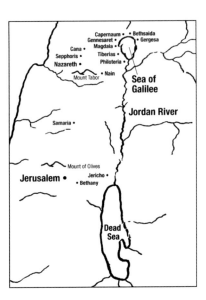

Jesus shared a lot of cool stuff with His disciples that night in the upper room, besides the fact that He loved them and expected them to lead as servant leaders. He tells them once again that He will be leaving them but not to be afraid, that He is leaving to prepare a place for them. He tells them to remember that He is the way, the truth and the life (John 14:6). He shares what the role of the coming Holy Spirit will be in their lives and much, much more. Come and take a look.

Read: John 14:1-17:26; Luke 22:39-46; Matthew 26:36-46; Mark 14:32-42.

What do we know about how Jesus prayed in the garden? (Matt. 26:36-46; Mark 14:32-42; Luke 22:39-46)

What lessons about prayer is Jesus modeling?

How were the disciples responding during this time?

What other questions do you still have?

Outside the Box

What a night! Jesus is going back over a lot of what He has been teaching these leaders over the past three and a half years of investing in them, as well as telling them new things. There is a little bit of everything here. One thing that I do not want you to miss is Jesus' incredibly instructive illustration to sum up many of the things He has been talking about. He likens leadership in the movement to a vineyard. He says the Father is a vinedresser, Jesus is the vine and we are the branches to bear the fruit of the Holy Spirit in our lives. He lays out for us each person's role in the process. God's job as the vinedresser is to wash and prune, Jesus' job as vine is to provide the life-giving nourishment to the branches, the Holy Spirit's job is to bear fruit and our job is to abide on the vine. Sometimes we want to do God's job, Jesus' job or the Holy Spirit's job. Our job makes us feel very unimportant. Our job is to simply remain, or abide, in Jesus, the vine, and allow the fruit of the Holy Spirit to develop on our branches. Leaders, your number one job is to remain in Jesus. Stay connected to the vine or you cannot bear any spiritual fruit. The fruit comes as you get into the word of God, spend time with the Father, get close to the Bridegroom and listen to His voice. If you want to bear fruit for the kingdom — abide in Jesus. The fruit that you bear will last, and it will be in proportion to the abiding you are doing.

He then warns them one last time of the coming persecution. With this, they sing a song and head across the valley and up the Mount of Olives (Matt. 26:30). Jesus takes them to a place they were familiar with, because each day He would go there after a hard day in the temple preaching. He takes them to the quiet of a garden called Gethsemane, on the lower slope of the Mount of Olives. There, Jesus once again takes Peter, James and John, the leaders of the leaders, a little deeper into the garden and tells them to stay awake, keep watch and pray that they would not fall into temptation. He goes about a stone's throw further, kneels down and begins to talk with the Father. In deep agony, He begins to sweat drops of blood. He prays, *"'Abba, Father,' he said, "everything is possible for you. Take this cup from me. Yet not what I will, but what You will'"* (Mark 14:36). The disciples must have heard this part of the prayer — maybe Jesus was screaming it in agony — or maybe they asked Him after He rose from the dead: "Remember back in the garden when you were praying, Jesus? What were you saying to the Father and what was His response?" We do not know when the disciples discovered the essence of the conversation between the Father and the Son, but when they did hear, it made a lasting impression on them. Jesus was saying, *"not my will but yours be done."* These are the same words God waits each day to hear from you and me. Each moment of each day the Father waits for us to yield our wills, to release control and allow Jesus to live through us. The overwhelming teaching of the Apostle Paul is that Jesus is in me to live through me.

Jesus gets up from His praying and goes to check on His leaders, and they are fast asleep. It has been a long day and they are exhausted. Jesus wakes them up and encourages them to watch and pray so that they will not fall in the moment of temptation. He then returns and keeps praying, *"'My Father, if it is not possible for this cup to be taken away unless I drink it, may your will be done'"* (Matt. 26:42). We see God the Son desiring a different will than God the Father, yet the Son submits to the will of the Father. He went back again and they were once again sleeping. At that very moment, Judas, leading a crowd of people with clubs and swords, comes marching up to seize Jesus and take Him away to be judged.

The Submissive Son

"'Father, if you are willing, take this cup from me; yet not my will, but yours be done.'"

Luke 22:42

Personal Notes

SEEING GOD

Live It Out

Each moment of each day the Father waits for us to yield our wills to His will. He longs to hear us say, "Father, not my will, but yours be done in my life!" Spend some time with your disciples talking about what it means to give up your will for the will of God and how one does this daily.

Other Thoughts

Digging Deeper

John 15:10-14

Romans 5:19

Romans 16:26

Ephesians 5:15-21

Hebrews 13:17

James 4:6-10

1 Peter 1:22

DAY 47 | Crucified Leadership

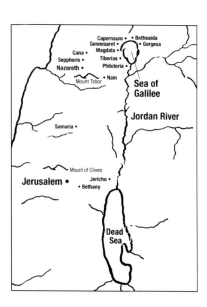

Jesus is identified to the crowd of people who have come to take Him away by Judas, who has come to betray Him. Judas kisses Jesus, and Jesus responds by calling him *"Friend"* (Matt. 26:50). He was a friend of sinners until the end! Betrayed into the hands of the religious leaders, Jesus is led away to be questioned, lied about, treated unjustly, beaten, whipped and, finally, to be hung on a cross between two criminals.

Read: Luke 23:26-49; Matthew 27:27-56; Mark 15:16-41; John 19:13-30.

As you read these passages, list all the ways in which Jesus suffered for us.

What is Jesus modeling for us about leadership?

As you reread the crucifixion story, what new insights do you discover?

What questions do you still have?

King of the Jews

"The written notice of the charge against him read: THE KING OF THE JEWS."

Mark 15:26

Personal Notes

Outside the Box

There is not much I can say about the death of Jesus that has not been said hundreds of times, written about and put up on the big screen. The obvious is that Jesus suffered in His humanity greatly in those last few hours. What may not be so obvious is how He suffered spiritually. He told His disciples the night before, *"'My soul is overwhelmed with sorrow to the point of death'"* (Matt. 26:38). Maybe the greatest suffering Jesus experienced was when He cried out, *"'My God, my God, why have you forsaken me?'"* (Matt. 27:46). God the Father, at that moment, had placed all of our sin on Jesus, for it is written, *"'But he was pierced for our transgressions, he was crushed for our iniquities; the punishment that brought us peace was upon him, and by his wounds we are healed"* (Isa. 53:5). I think one of the biggest ways Jesus suffered was being forsaken by the Father, who had to turn His back on Him because He was carrying all the weight of our sin. His Father could no longer look at Him. Once for all time, the sacrifice had been made. The Passover Lamb of God had His blood shed and the veil of the temple was torn. Because of that sacrifice and that entrance into the holiest place in the temple, we now have access to the living God, face-to-face access to the throne room of heaven. Those who believe are adopted into this new family and have unlimited access into the presence of the Holy of Holies. Unbelievable!

The author of Hebrews puts it like this: *"Therefore brothers, since we have confidence to enter the Most Holy Place by the blood of Jesus, by a new and living way opened for us through the curtain, that is, his body, and since we have a great priest over the house of God, let us draw near to God with a sincere heart in full assurance of faith"* (Heb. 10:19-22). Because of Jesus' sacrifice as the Lamb of God, we can now come to God our Father spotless, because Jesus took our spots and washed them white as snow. The place that was once forbidden to enter, the Holy of Holies, was now made available to all through Jesus' sacrifice on the cross. How can it be that my God would die for me? It was the great exchange: I had a debt I could not pay; He paid a debt He did not owe. Jesus lived out His love as an example to us, because *"Greater love has no one than this, that he lay down his life for his friends"* (John 15:13). He laid down His life for you and me! You and I are considered friends, worthy of that sacrifice. In that moment, the innocent died for the guilty, the holy for the unholy. He died for us!

I also want to remind you that not only did Jesus suffer for you at the end of His life, but He suffered His whole life for you. We've looked at this, but it's good to remember what we've learned over the past weeks. Think about it. In heaven, Jesus was worshipped all the time by angels that adored Him. He was obeyed and believed in all the time there. As the greatest missionary ever, He left all that and came to Earth to be hated, disobeyed, mistreated, rejected and killed. The will of the Father was for Jesus to die on the cross. It was not the will of the Son, but Jesus was willing to submit to the will of the Father to show us the extent of His love. You see, the will of the Father is the same for us as it was for Jesus. The will of the Father is that we die to ourselves. This is the will of God for you that you die daily (1 Cor. 15:31). Paul said, *"I have been crucified with Christ and I no longer live, but Christ lives in me"* (Gal. 2:20). When we follow Jesus and Paul's examples, we exchange our sinful, self-centered lives for His holy, pure, glorious life. What an exchange! Are you willing to die to yourself? Are you willing to submit yourself to the will of the Father?

Live It Out

Leadership Jesus-style is a leadership that dies to one's own desires, passions and dreams and submits to the will of the Father. Have you died to yourself? Spend some time meditating on the verses in Digging Deeper and see how Paul did it. The overwhelming message of the Apostle Paul is death to self and life in Christ Jesus. Talk with some disciples about this today.

Other Thoughts

Digging Deeper

Isaiah 53:5-12

Romans 6:1-14

Romans 8:9-11

1 Corinthians 15:31

Galatians 2:20

Galatians 5:24-25

Galatians 6:14-18

Philippians 1:21

Philippians 3:7-11

Hebrews 12:3-4

DAY 48 | Resurrection Leadership

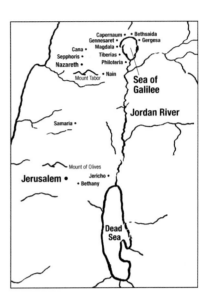

After laying His life down for you and me, two men come to retrieve His body and prepare it for burial. One is Joseph of Arimathea and the other is our friend Nicodemus. As you read today, take special note of these two men. The Lord is risen indeed!

Read: John 19:31-20:31; Luke 23:50-24:49; Matthew 27:57-28:15; Mark 15:42-16:18.

As you study these passages, list all of the verses that describe the mental attitude of the disciples.

Why is the resurrection so important to the Christian faith (1 Cor. 15:1-19)?

Because of the resurrection of Jesus, what is now true about the life of Jesus?

What questions do you still have?

Outside the Box

He has risen from the dead! Death could not hold Him down. Jesus, my Savior, triumphed over death and rose in victory. The Bible says that with Jesus' resurrection, *"'Death has been swallowed up in victory.' 'Where, O death, is your victory? Where, O death, is your sting? The sting of death is sin, and the power of sin is the law. But thanks be to God! He gives us the victory through our Lord Jesus Christ'"* (1 Cor. 15:54-57). The power to live life is in the power of Jesus' victory over death. Jesus rose as the first of many who will rise: *"Now if we died with Christ, we believe that we shall also live with him. For we know that since Christ was raised from the dead, he cannot die again; death no longer has mastery over him. The death he died, he died to sin once for all; but the life he lives, he lives to God. In the same way, count yourselves dead to sin but alive to God in Christ Jesus"* (Rom. 6:8-11). That is powerful! That is the resurrection of Jesus — it gives us the power to defeat sin in our lives as we yield ourselves to the transforming work of the Father. The power of Jesus and His resurrection flows through us as we set aside our will and allow Jesus to live in and through us.

Resurrection leadership is leadership that is allowing Jesus to live in and through oneself. The servant leader, the submissive leader, the passionate leader, the effective leader is the someone who has Jesus in them, living through them. Leadership, Jesus-style, is a radically different type of leadership than what our world models for us. Worldly leadership is a self-absorbed, control-oriented leadership that presses the will of the leader onto the people. It lords itself over them, controls and is demanding, harsh and cruel. Jesus-style leadership is gentle, kind, loving, compassionate, slow to anger, abounding in loving kindness and grace-filled. Which kind of leader do you want to be?

Speaking of leaders, what did you discover about Joseph and Nicodemus? Joseph was a member of the ruling Council, a good and righteous man. Nicodemus was a Pharisee who had come to Jesus by night. We discover these two leaders in Israel were secret disciples (John 19:38). They were undercover Christ-followers, who believed that Jesus was the Messiah, but hid their beliefs for fear of the Jews. Their fear immobilized them and kept their faith a secret. They were afraid of suffering for the name of Jesus or damaging their reputation among the religious crowd. Do you know any undercover disciples? Are you an undercover Christ-follower? What are you afraid of? What if people found out that you were a Jesus follower? He publicly went to the cross for me and yet, at times, I still find it so hard to stand for Him. To my own embarrassment, there are times when I have not stood up for the One who gave everything for me. I know I am not alone. But, we must remember that there is nothing this world has to offer that even comes close to knowing Jesus — nothing!

Live It Out

Are you an undercover Christ-follower? Make a commitment to stand for Jesus and you will feel His resurrection power flow through you. Speak His name and tell others of His sacrifice. Spend some time talking with your disciples about what fears they have in making it known that they love Jesus. Pray for one another that together you would make Jesus known.

The Resurrection

"Jesus said to her, 'I am the resurrection and the life. He who believes in me will live, even though he dies…'"

John 11:25

Personal Notes

SEEING GOD

Other Thoughts

Digging Deeper

Acts 2:29-35

1 Corinthians 15:1-58

Ephesians 2:4-10

Philippians 3:10-16

1 Peter 1:3-9

1 John 5:3-5

DAY 49 | Shepherd Leadership

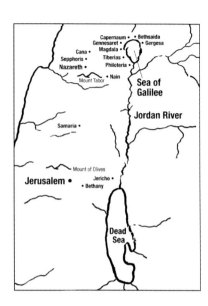

After rising from the dead, Jesus appears to His disciples on several occasions. Paul lists the appearances in 1 Corinthians 15:3-8. He appeared to many people individually — to His leaders on several occasions and even to a group of disciples numbering more than 500. On one of these appearances Jesus repeats a miracle that had changed Peter's life early in the ministry. This is the last breakfast with Jesus. See what instructions Jesus gives about being a leader!

Read: John 21:1-25.

As you read this story, how do you think the disciples were feeling? What failures had they recently experienced?

What is Jesus modeling for us about leadership?

What does Jesus expect from His leaders?

What other questions do you still have?

Foundation

"For no one can lay any foundation other than the one already laid, which is Jesus Christ."

1 Corinthians 3:11

Personal Notes

Outside the Box

Jesus has already met with His leaders two times in Jerusalem behind closed doors (John 21:14), because they are scared to death of the religious leaders and the Roman guard, who are looking to wipe out the Jesus' movement. Jesus tells them to head back down to Galilee and wait for Him (Matt. 28:10). They head north to Peter's house on the Sea of Galilee. Peter gets tired of waiting and decides to try his luck at his old profession — fishing. He invites those who are there waiting to come along. They fished all night and caught nothing. Sound familiar, like in Luke 5? Jesus prepares a breakfast of fish and bread for them on the shore as day breaks and, when they are close enough, He calls out to them, "Catch anything?" They answer "No!" in frustration. Jesus then tells them, *"'Throw your net on the right side of the boat and you will find some'"* (John 21:6). They do and, lo and behold, 153 fish are hauled in. John looks at Peter and says, "Hey man, there is only one person who could make this happen." Peter grabs his tunic and dives into the water and swims for shore to embrace Jesus, while the others drag the net full of fish to shore. They all gather and enjoy an early morning breakfast, Jesus' last breakfast with them. When they finish, they get up and Jesus leads them on a walk down the beach.

As they walk Jesus asks Peter a series of questions that at first glance all look the same. In fact, Peter's answers all kind of sound the same. They are not though. You have to keep in mind that it has been weeks now since Jesus has risen from the dead. He has come to them two times as a group. Jesus gently comes to Peter, the head leader and says to him, *"Simon* [indicating his life before he met Jesus] *son of John, do you truly love* [agape] *me more than these?"* Jesus uses the Greek word for love "agape," which was the strongest form of love — a sold-out, unconditional love, the type of love that took Jesus to the cross. Peter says back to Jesus, *"Yes, Lord…you know that I love* [phileo] *you."* Notice, Simon changes the word to "phileo," which is the Greek word for brotherly love, a very human love between close friends. Jesus responds by saying, *"Feed my lambs."* Who were Jesus' lambs? And who were the *"these"* that Jesus refers to in the initial question? The *"these"* must have been the fish that they had just caught lying dead in the sand. I think Jesus was asking Peter, "Am I more important to you than these fish and all they represent — your business, your vocation and your reputation as a great fisherman? If so, get to work, telling the lost lambs of the world about me. Tend to them. If you love Me, you will obey Me."

As they walk a little farther, Jesus gently asks again, *"Simon son of John, do you truly love* [agape] *me?"* Peter responds, *"Yes, Lord, you know that I love* [phileo] *you."* Jesus responds, *"Take care of my sheep."* I think Jesus was here saying to Peter, "I need you to step up to the plate and get to work shepherding the followers and disciples in the movement. But you are not doing it right now — if you love Me, you will get to My work."

Jesus then asks, *"Simon son of John, do you love* [phileo] *me?"* Peter frustrated, responds, *"Lord, you know all things; you know that I love* [phileo] *you."* Jesus said *"Feed my sheep,"* but I think He meant, "The lambs and the sheep of the world need you to lead them. Let's go! Get your eyes off of yourself and on me. In your flesh, as Simon, you can do nothing, but I can do it through you if you will only take your eyes off of yourself and walk by faith. Look, I can provide for all your needs. You fished all night and caught nothing and at my word you pulled in 153 fish in seconds. I am big and I can do anything. If you say you love [phileo] Me, obey me." Wow! What a lesson for Peter. This is the last we read or hear of Peter going back to fishing. Jesus tells Peter to lead the disciples (probably some 500) to a mountain where He will appear to them next. What will happen?

Live It Out

How about you? Do you "phileo" or "agape" Jesus? If you love Him, you will obey Him! I am not sure why Peter was so reluctant to use the word "agape" in his relationship with Jesus. Maybe because he had already said that he would die for Him and then denied he even knew Jesus three times. Maybe he was second-guessing his ability in the flesh to love Jesus. Spend some time talking with your disciples about obedience and shepherding Jesus' lambs and sheep.

Other Thoughts

Digging Deeper

Psalms 23:1-6

Psalms 78:70-72

Jeremiah 3:15-16

Ezekiel 34:1-31

John 10:1-18

Acts 20:27-35

Hebrews 13:20,21

1 Peter 5: 1-9

DAY 50 | Obedient Leadership

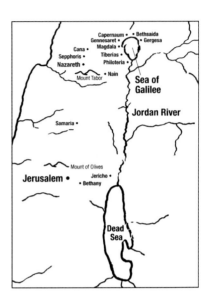

Peter leads a large group of disciples to an isolated (perhaps secretive) meeting where Jesus will once again give them their marching orders. Then they make their way back to Jerusalem to await the coming Holy Spirit as the movement switches into its next phase of multiplication. Let's take a look at these last two meetings with the disciples.

Read: Matthew 28:16-20; Mark 16:19-20; Luke 24:50-53; Acts 1:1-11.

What were the marching orders of Jesus (Matt. 28:16-20)?

What role did the Holy Spirit now play in Jesus' absence (Acts 1:1-11)?

Why do you think the ascension was important to Jesus?

When and where will we see Jesus again (Zech. 14:4-9)?

What other questions do you still have?

Outside the Box

Peter leads the group to the mountain and they find Jesus waiting. They worship Him as the risen Savior of the world. It is here on this mountain in Galilee, where Jesus had asked them to come (Matt. 28:16), that Jesus sums up His life's work and gives them one simple command — **to make disciples.** That's right; the command is not to "Go" but to "make disciples." There is only one major command in this verse and there are three main verbs. Let me walk you through it. The first verb is "go," which has the idea of "as you go." Thus, Jesus is basically saying to the disciples, "as you go through life, make disciples." As we walk through our daily activities of life, we need to make it our goal to invest in others, telling them the Good News of who Jesus is. Tell people that He is the way to God the Father (John 14:6). This is called evangelism. Jesus also says that this idea of making disciples is for all nations. It is transcultural; it is for the whole world. The gospel is for everyone, regardless of race, creed, color or religious background. The movement of disciple making, Jesus-style, is to span the globe. The second verb is to "baptize." Remember, baptism is Jesus' day was a form of identification. Thus, we are to help people identify with Jesus, His message and His mission. This is called edifying. The last verb is to "teach." Teach everything that Jesus commanded. Remember Jesus told us that if we love Him, we will do what He says. This is called equipping. Thus, we are called to make disciples by doing three things: 1) We are called to evangelize the lost; 2) to edify the believer; and 3) to equip the disciple in a lifestyle of obeying Jesus and devoting their lives to making disciples who can make disciples in turn.

This making of disciples fulfills a new commandment — to love one another, so that by our love all the world will know that we are His (John 13:34-35). A disciple is known by his/her supernatural love. It is a lifestyle of loving God and loving others, a lifestyle that is Christ-centered, not me centered.

This making of disciples happens as we walk through life. A second command is given in this passage in the small Greek word "idou." It is usually translated as "behold" or "lo." It simply means that as we go through life, we need to keep our eyes on Jesus — for He is with us always, even to the end of the age! If you are a college student, be conscious as you walk to and from classes throughout your day and make it the priority to invest in others, telling them that Jesus is the way, the truth and the life. This is the lifestyle Jesus is looking for, not a program or a religion. If you work at a job, share Jesus with the coworkers and clients. Tell them that Jesus is the way. Every day you encounter someone, you have a chance to evangelize, edify or equip. Live a Jesus-like lifestyle in front of others. Keep your eyes on Him. Make it your passion to **make disciples.**

This is not rocket science — it is easy to understand, but very hard to prioritize. When you start making disciples and stop playing at church, your life may just turn upside down. Satan will do everything to get you to focus on yourself and not on Jesus. Even though Jesus' strategy for making disciples is simple to understand, at times, it seems impossible to do. That is why Jesus left us with a promise, *"I am with you always."* Our only hope is to die to self and allow Jesus to make disciples through us. That is the exchanged life, your life for His life, death to self so that Jesus might live in us (Gal. 2:20). It is the mystery that Paul talks about: *"Christ in you"* (Col.1:27).

Cornerstone

"Consequently, you are ... God's household built on the foundation of the apostles and prophets, with Christ Jesus himself as the chief cornerstone."

Ephesians 2:20

Personal Notes

SEEING GOD

Live It Out

From this mountaintop experience He leads the team back to Jerusalem and then out to Bethany. On the Mount of Olives, he tells them, *"'But you will receive power when the Holy Spirit comes on you; and you will be my witnesses in Jerusalem, and in all Judea and Samaria, and to the ends of the earth'"* (Acts 1:8). We are witnesses of the person and work of Jesus Christ. We are His disciples who love Him and prove that love by obeying Him. He then ascends to heaven, like the king who left for a short while, leaving the servants with ten minas and telling them to go do business for Him. He too will return and each will have to give an account of how they did with the job that they were given. How will it go with you when Jesus returns or calls you home to heaven?

When Jesus returns to claim His rightful kingdom, will He find you making disciples? Will He find you living for yourself, playing church or will you be dying to self and living for Him? The daily choice is yours. Choose life because Jesus is life, and you will live. May He find you faithfully making disciples that will in turn make more disciples! Don't stop meeting with those you have been investing in. Make a plan to go deeper in understanding who Jesus is. Go back through this study with another friend and make another disciple.

Other Thoughts

Digging Deeper

Ephesians 1:18-23

Philippians 2:9-11

Hebrews 2:8-10

Hebrews 9:23-29

Hebrews 12:1-3

Revelation 5:1-14

Zechariah 8:3

Zechariah 14:4, 8-9

Notes

Notes